Grow It.
Eat It.

Grow It.

Eat It.

by

Linda Larson

illustrations by

Jessie Johnson

photographs by
Arlene Gardinier

ISBN: 1-932472-33-9

Illustrated by Jessica Allen Johnson
Photographs by Arlene Gardinier

Acknowledgements

This book was a group effort. Arlene and Jessie, this book would not exist without you; thanks for a wonderful book-creating experience.

Thanks to those who shared their recipes: Del Brill, Sue Brill, Virginia Brill, Kirsten Clark, Duane Erickson, Louise Erickson, Marlyne Erickson, Arlene Gardinier, Trish Gardinier-Vos, Marian Guss, Jessie Johnson, Mona Ketzeback, Earl Larson, Mary Larson, Rosemary Larson, Lisa Ramsbacher, Marcella Ramsbacher, and Sandy Westling

Designed and edited by John Toren

Nodin Press is a division of Micawber's, Inc.
530 N 3rd Street,
Suite 120
Minneapolis, MN 55401

Dedication

To Robert and Hannah
– L. L.

To My Family
– J. J.

Duane and Ryan
Trish and Jeff
Henry and Hermione
– A. G.

Radishes / Rutabagas / Shallots / Squash: Winter and Summer
Tomatillos / Tomatoes / Turnips

Culinary Herbs   96

Basil / Chervil / Chives /Cilantro (Coriander)
Dill / Marjoram / Oregano / Parsley
Rosemary / Sage / Savory / Tarragon / Thyme

Medicinal Herbs   106

Anise / Bee Balm / Borage / Calendula
Catnip / Chamomile / Echinacea (Purple Coneflower)
Feverfew / Horehound / Hyssop
Lavender / Lemon Balm / Mint
Nasturtium / Valerian

Wild Things   112

Black Walnut / Crab Apples / Chokecherries
Cranberries / Currants and gooseberries / Dandelion
Elderberries / Fiddlehead Ferns / Grapes
Hazelnuts / Hawthorn / Lamb's Quarters
Nettle / Plantain / Plum / Red Clover
Rose / Wood Sorrel / Yarrow

Flowers 122

Challenges for the Expert Gardener 134

Helpful Resources 141

Introduction

How to Use This Book

This book has essential information for both novice and expert gardeners. And just what does a gardener do with a bountiful harvest? I've got some answers with some easy and tasty recipes. We hope the lovely photos and art work on these pages will inspire people to get messy in the garden and the kitchen.

Each part contains complete information on how to grow and cook each kind of fruit, vegetable, herb, and flower in this book. Planting advice is specifically for cooler zones three and four. Though gardening seems simple enough, these pages include each plant's specific needs.

In this book, you will find many ideas for cooking fresh veggies, fruits, and herbs. I created these many recipes for people like myself, tired at the end of a busy day, looking though the garden for something fresh, and then trying to find a fast and healthy way to cook it. So these easy and everyday recipes focus on the harvest and include ingredients that are already in the cupboard or found at most grocery stores. I've substituted milk for cream and olive oil for butter as well as other adaptations to make the food healthier. Of course, some recipes are best when decadent and I've left them that way.

This book combines growing and cooking in one handy place. Not only will new gardeners and new cooks enjoy this book, but recipes abound for expert gardeners who may be overwhelmed by the garden's bountiful harvest. Additional information shows how wonderfully useful and healthy our garden produce is. I've included information about what an astute observer might find in the woods, such as chokecherries and wild plums.

Gardening and cooking are great hobbies, both calling for creativity and both offering fine fruits of labor. Fresh food out of the garden is divine. Once a person tastes a lettuce picked minutes before it's served, or beans straight from the vine, it's tough to go back to stuff out of the can, the freezer, or the store. Perhaps hell is being forced to eat soggy canned peas for eternity, while watching someone in heaven eat fresh peas right off the vine.

In any case, I hope you enjoy reading and using *Grow It. Eat It.* as much as I've enjoyed gardening and writing this book.

Recipe for Good Soil

I'm about to divulge the ultimate secret that every good gardener knows. What exactly is the trick to extra juicy tomatoes and thick, sweet carrots and plump peas? Good soil. Minnesota has a range of soil problems from clay to sand, but they can all be solved with one item – compost. A heavy clay soil has better drainage with the addition of organic matter and light sandy soil holds moisture better. A gardener won't need heavy doses of chemical fertilizers if the soil is rich with compost. And the plants love it! They are healthier, which means no need for chemical pesticides or fungicides. Composting might take a little extra time, but it's cheaper and healthier than chemicals.

So what's compost and how do we get some? Compost is garden waste rotted into humus, organic matter that is crumbly and full of nutrients for plants. Some gardening catalogs and stores sell compost at exorbitant rates (understandably, compost's nickname "black gold"). But by using stuff we have around the yard and house, we can make compost for free.

Here's how it works. By mixing different yard and kitchen wastes, microorganisms break down the mixture into a rich humus. It's a good idea to combine dried material (leaves) with fresh material (grass clippings). Mix in a little soil from your garden, which helps add microorganisms. A compost pile also needs air and water. The best way to do that is to stir the pile frequently and water it once in a while. A well-tended compost pile will not stink.

One way to build a compost pile is to dump stuff in a heap and let it rot. A compost bin, hand-made or store-bought, also works well. It helps to separate the compost into two piles—an "old" pile (one almost ready for use) and a "new" pile (the place to dump kitchen scraps, etc.). Some people like three bins for the different stages of compost. However you decide to make it, compost is ready when it looks like dirt, crumbly and black.

Here's what to put in the compost pile. Hint: Shredding and chopping helps the stuff break down faster.

Leaves	Grass
Coffee Grounds	Egg Shells (shells only)
Weeds	Fruit and Vegetable Peels
Cow, Chicken, or Horse Manure	

Important note: Due to some nasty bacteria, the current recommendation is to let manure compost first before using it in the garden or apply it 120 days before harvesting food crops.

Here's what to avoid.

Meat	Oils or Fats
Bones	Human or Pet Waste
Weed Seeds	Diseased Plants
Leftovers from meals	

These things don't break down well, may encourage disease, and often attract rodents. If the compost pile gets hot enough, the heat will kill weed seeds and diseased plants (but it's got to get really hot).

What if there's just no space for a compost pile in a tiny garden? Or what if it seems like too much work? Well, try burying compost-related items. Dig some shredded leaves or grass clippings into the soil in the fall. My grandfather, a true Minnesota fisherman, dug the leftover fish guts and heads deeply into the unused garden spaces so that the next spring my grandmother had a wonderfully fertile garden spot.

For homemade liquid fertilizer, try compost tea. Take some finished compost, add some water, and let it steep. Use the compost tea for watering the garden.

Advice for Beginners: Planning an Organic Garden

Okay, you've always wanted a garden, but you don't know where to begin. My advice is to start small. If the idea of digging up sod seems like too much work, try gardening in pots. Or if the idea of gardening at all is intimidating, visit your local farmer's market for fresh fruits and vegetables. After being a participant in a farmer's market, I found most growers used organic methods and knowledgably answered questions about both growing and cooking their produce. I also learned from my customers as well. A farmer's market is a great place to try something before you grow it, too.

Find a spot that gets plenty of sunlight, about 6 mid-day hours. I live in a woodsy spot, but I still get enough light in my garden, though my flowers bloom a few days later than open spaces nearby. Some vegetables can grow with less sunlight (lettuce and carrots) but some need lots of light (tomatoes and peppers).

It's a good idea to remove sod when beginning a new garden. Some people like to till it into the ground, but I prefer removing it since I don't till the garden regularly. (In my experience, grass grows everywhere but where you want it to grow.) If the garden space is covered in weeds, watch out for *poison ivy*. My husband, not realizing what poison ivy looked like, found out how allergic he was to it only after working in it. Watch for three, shiny jagged leaves. Remember that the leaves, the stems, the berries, and the roots all cause a rash. Burning the plants release the oils in the air. Spraying can control it, but I've found the only way to keep it from coming back is to cover myself from head to toe and pull the thing up by the roots (very carefully, I might add).

Before digging, check where the utility lines are.

Plants grow best in loose soil, so dig or till the dirt until it has a crumbly texture. Wait until the soil is sufficiently dry before trying this in the spring to avoid making the soil compacted. I tend to do the most garden work in the spring and in the fall. A little extra preparation helps me avoid lots of work later. I prepare my garden beds by digging them deeply to break up clumps of soil, removing rocks or large roots, and adding compost. Some people enjoy using a tiller to loosen the garden beds and dig in the compost. Part of my garden has raised beds, which is nice for extra drainage.

Soil can be tested for nitrogen, phosphorus and potassium, necessary nutrients for healthy plants. The Minnesota Cooperative Extension Service offers soil testing for gardeners. Soil tests can also be bought at stores and through garden catalogs. If you are beginning a new garden or have had problems in the garden, a soil test may be useful. Keep in mind that there are organic amendments available and the cheapest way to fix soil is to add compost.

If you garden in rows, plan so that each plant gets the maximum southern exposure. For example, plant small plants such as lettuces in front of taller and bushier plants. Other ideas to consider are adding height to your garden with trellises, poles, or fences. If your garden is short on space, try intensive gardening—plants clustered together rather than in rows. This works especially well with lettuces and herbs. When installing a perennial (a plant that comes back each year), plan for the mature size and fill in the extra space with annuals.

Rotating Crops

Different crops have different requirements. For example, corn needs plenty of nutrients whereas beans fix (make) their own nitrogen. By moving the crops around, there is less stress on the garden. Plan on at least a four-year rotation. Plants tend to become more vulnerable to diseases when they are planted in the same spot every year since certain types of plants get certain types of disease. For example, plant beans where the tomatoes were last year instead of peppers. I write down what I planted and where I planted it, placing those notes in the same spot every year so I can find them when I need them. This may seem like an obvious thing to do, but I did this after believing I could remember, only to be dumbfounded in the spring, when everything is the same color of mud.

Related crops:
1. Tomatoes, peppers, potatoes
2. Legumes
3. Onions, leeks, garlic
4. Cucumbers, melons, squash
5. Cabbage, broccoli, cauliflower

Timing It: What to Plant When

Cool weather crops often can take a bit of frost (though not a freeze—below 20 degrees F). The trick is to be sure the soil is ready. Grab a handful of garden soil and make a fist. If it crumbles, it's ready. If it's wet, muddy, or holds the shape of your hand, it's not; the plants or seeds may rot. Avoid working in the soil when it's too wet, because it will compact the soil. I am an anxious gardener and like to plant as soon as I can, so I prepare a garden bed in the fall, digging in compost and raking it smooth, so that I can plant as soon as the soil is ready in the spring. Cool weather crops are often done producing by the hot days of summer.

Frost will kill warm weather crops and often they won't grow well until the soil is warm. If I am worried about getting a special variety of warm weather plant, I often buy my plants early, keeping them on the porch during the day and bringing them in at night until the ground is warm.

Cool Weather Crops (plant these as soon as the soil is ready)

Broccoli	Radishes
Lettuce	Spinach
Peas and Peapods	

Warm Weather Crops (plant these only when the soil is warm)

Basil	Eggplant
Beans	Peppers
Beets	Squash
Cantaloupe	Tomatoes
Cucumbers	Watermelon

Hint: If frost is imminent, cover the garden with a cloth sheet (not plastic.)

The varieties recommended in this book will work in cooler climates and shorter growing seasons. Breeders develop hybrids with this in mind, as well as disease and pest resistance. The organic grower stays away from genetically modified seed, because of its untested results on our long term health and the long term health of the earth. Most of the recommendations are currently offered in seed catalogs (see the Helpful Resources section, p. 139). Every year new varieties are offered, so look for the early maturing ones. Also, try heirloom vegetables, whose seeds can be saved year after year.

I love being in my garden so I use watering as my excuse to get outside first thing in the morning. Mornings are better for watering since the heat of the day won't evaporate the moisture. Also, plants have a chance to dry before cool evenings can infect them with fungus. Gardens usually need about an inch of rain a week. A rain gauge helps me keep track.

Avoiding Weeds with Mulch

After planting my cool weather seeds and plants, I mulch between the rows and around the plants. The mulch keeps the soil cool and moist. Some people like to till between rows, but since I have raised garden beds, the soil doesn't become compact. The thicker the mulch, the fewer weeds I have later. I mulch the warm weather plants only after the soil is warm.

What should a gardener use for mulch? I use "recycled" straw, once used for growing mushrooms from a local mushroom grower. Compost is a good mulch, too, since it acts like a slow release fertilizer. Leaves and grass can be used as well. (Try to avoid anything that may have a lot of weed seeds.) These kinds of mulches break down and can be dug into the soil.

Black and red plastic mulches are also useful. Bark mulch is good around permanent plantings, such as perennial plants. Gravel can be used for a path, but plants tend to grow up through it and the tiny rocks may travel into the garden spaces.

Attracting Beneficial Insects

Since I don't like to use chemicals in my garden, I try to attract good bugs that prey on the bad bugs in my garden. The best way to do this is to plant dill, alyssum, cilantro, marigolds or other flowers or flowering herbs right in the garden along with other vegetables. My garden doesn't have perfect rows of vegetables, but I like to think it looks pretty with all the different colors and textures.

Also, avoid planting large areas of just one kind of plant. For example, I planted a 4 foot by 16 foot garden bed of lettuce and other greens one year, but I also planted peas on the west side to give the lettuce plants shade and extend their season a bit as well as dill around the perimeter to discourage bunnies and attract lady bugs.

Repelling Pests

Pests are creatures that get to my harvest before I do. Deer, mice, rabbits, squirrels and bad bugs are not welcome in my garden. So how do I get rid of them without the use of chemicals? There are many non-poisonous, easy-on-the-environment remedies available. Marigolds may repel nematodes and their odor may stave off some rodents. Animal pests may avoid dill, cilantro, garlic and other "smelly" herbs, so plant them around the perimeter of your garden. The only bean plants that survived one year were the ones planted next to peppery nasturtiums. I sprinkle cayenne pepper (bought in bulk from the grocery store) around my tomato plants before they begin to ripen and it seems to keep the squirrels and chipmunks away.

A fragrant soap, such as Irish Spring, placed strategically around the garden, or in bushes or trees, may work, too. Blood meal, a by-product of animals, sprinkled around the garden may also deter some animals. Some garden catalogs offer bobcat or cougar urine. Be sure to replace the smelly things after rain.

Perhaps the most obvious though most time-consuming thing to do is build a fence. If deterring burrowing creatures is the goal, be sure to dig the fence into the ground. If deterring deer is the goal, be sure it is high enough so they don't leap over it, perhaps 5 feet.

When I let my guard down, a chipmunk may get the ripe strawberry before I do, or a deer may chomp on my bean plants, but these solutions keep away animals that aren't starving. In fact, a bunny surprised me by munching on a dandelion even though she sat near my bean plants. Later I found a nest of five baby rabbits in the mulch next to my potatoes. I like that wildlife and I can co-exist in my garden.

Sometimes a pest may get out of control, and co-existence seems too Pollyanna-ish. It's time for the organic gardener to get tough! To remove aphids, use a hose to spray water on the undersides of leaves to remove them. Handpick Mexican bean beetles or Colorado potato beetles, checking under leaves to remove their eggs. Collect them in a jar of soapy water, which is much easier than crushing them. Buy ladybugs or praying mantises to release into your garden. Sometimes I choose to lose a battle: for example, I allow caterpillars to eat my purple coneflowers in order to enjoy the butterflies. Remember that spraying insecticides not only kills the pests, but also the predators, sometimes creating a bigger problem.

If it's tough to tell what exactly is wrong in the garden or the kitchen, some expert advice may be needed. In Minnesota, useful information can be found from your local University of Minnesota Extension Service office. Be sure to request information for organic solutions to your gardening problems. Their web address is *www.extension.umn.edu.* They have offices all over the state staffed with Master Gardeners who can answer questions about your specific area. They also have the Yard and Garden Line at 1-888-624-4771 (612-624-4771 in the metro), which is free except for talking to a staff member or submitting a sample. If you don't have web access, you can call the Info-U hotline at 1-800-525-8638 (612-624-2200 in the metro) for pre-recorded messages or to request facts sheets sent by fax.

My Personal Advice

Most of us have seen the magazines and tv shows with perfect flowers and perfect vegetables in perfect recipes. Well, my garden has weeds and my kitchen is messy.

And only those who can afford a professional gardener (or who garden for a living) will have perfect gardens. My goal is to have fresh food and lovely flowers. I try not to worry if something isn't going as well as planned. We can blame our failures on the weather and claim successes as our own. My garden flourishes when I have the time and the weather cooperates. I love to experiment, sometimes coaxing a zone five plant to grow in the cool zone four weather.

My advice to gardeners is to relax and enjoy! Most of us are lucky enough to afford food from the grocery store or a farmers' market so we shouldn't get stressed out about a garden. For everyday worries, however, I find that pulling weeds is a great way for me to relieve stress. A daily walk through the garden is refreshing, provided I'm not running from mosquitoes. And I love letting the "weeds" grow to see what kind of flowers they have. I've had some pleasant surprises.

Have fun in the garden!

Fruits

I love fresh fruit—bare, naked, and plain. Maybe it goes back to survival of the fittest, but ripe fruit off the tree, bush, vine or stem recalls an instinct to eat! fast! before the other critters get to it! Of course, a whole tree full of ripe fruit can baffle even the most seasoned cook, so I've included some ideas for saving and savoring fruit.

First, some quick tips.

• in most recipes, the berries are interchangeable, and pears and apples are interchangeable…experiment to find the best flavor combinations.

• serve berries over waffles, French toast, pancakes, ice cream, yogurt, or cereal.

• slice fruits and sprinkle with sugar to create juices.

• squeeze lemon juice over sliced apples or pears to prevent browning.

• arrange sliced fruit on a plate for a colorful appetizer or dessert.

• share the extra harvest with grateful friends and neighbors.

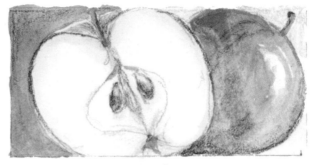

Apples

Looking for a fresh and tasty Minnesota apple in January? Try Honeycrisp; not only does it store well, it's sweet and crispy…and it sells out fast at farmers' markets and grocery stores. Other good storing apples are the tart Haralson, the milder Prairie Spy, and the appropriately named Keepsake. For cooking, try Northwestern Greening and Mantet. For fresh eating, try McIntosh and Sweet Sixteen. Cortland, which resists browning when cut, is a good choice for drying. Consider dwarf varieties, which take less space. Plant two similarly maturing fruit trees for cross-pollination.

Planting: Apple trees need attention: pruning in the early spring, spraying for insects and diseases during the season (organic products are available), and protecting the tree during the winter. For pruning, trim dead and damaged wood any time of year, but early spring (February and March) is best for shaping the tree. Trim any branches that cross each other and others that seem needed to open up the tree for light and air. For insects, try fake red apples, covered in a sticky goo (such as Tangle Trap), to capture the bugs before they lay their eggs in the fruit. For winter protection, wrap the tree trunk, starting at the very bottom to prevent mice and voles from chewing on the bark, and finishing as high as possible to minimize sunscald from the winter sun's glare on the snow.

Some of the reasons that apple trees don't bear fruit could be a late frost that kills early buds, a stressful previous summer or fall (for example, a drought), a lack of pollination (meaning the bees aren't around), a particularly heavy fruiting year previously, lack of cross pollination (meaning that two varieties with similar blooming dates need to be planted near each other), or the variety takes a long time to mature before it bears fruit.

Plant each tree following the instructions from the nursery: Dig a large hole, mounding loose soil on the bottom, placing the tree carefully in the hole, and filling loose soil around the tree, watering carefully. Plant trees 25 feet apart, though dwarf varieties can be closer.

Thinning: For larger apples, thin the apples five to eight inches apart soon after the blossom petals fall from the tree.

Harvesting: Different apples have different maturing times. Mantet matures in mid-August; McIntosh in mid-September; Haralson, Prairie Spy, Sweet Sixteen and Honeycrisp in late September; Cortland and Northwestern Greening in early October; Keepsake in mid-October.

Look for apples that have yellowish tinge in their background. Redness does not indicate how ripe the fruit is. Pull the apple and stem carefully from the spur.

Preparing: Apples are delicious fresh. For a quick applesauce, chop the apples (with or without the skins). Cook them until soft in a pan with just enough water so the apples don't stick to the bottom. Serve warm. Add cinnamon or sugar, if desired.

Storing: Apples keep best in the refrigerator. Those with bruises or broken skin should be used immediately. Apples are best canned as applesauce. Applesauce freezes well, too. To freeze apple slices, prepare the apples (wash, peel, core and slice). Dip them in lemon juice to prevent browning. Measure the slices needed for a recipe (for example, 6 cups for apple pie) and freeze in a container. Don't thaw the slices, but add a little extra time for cooking, or a little extra thickener for the liquid from the frozen slices.

Helpful Hint: To prevent apples from turning brown after being cut, dip the pieces in lemon juice or store-bought ascorbic or citric acid.

A Healthy Dose: One medium apple has 80 calories and 3.7 grams of fiber as well as 159 milligrams of potassium and 8 milligrams of vitamin C.

Historical Notes: The Romans were fond of apples and probably helped spread the fruit across Europe and Asia, though apples may have originated in Asia Minor. Early American settlers brought cultivated apples from England. Johnny Appleseed, aka Johnny Chapman, won his fame by planting apple seeds across America.

Recipes

Baked Apple Slices in Brown Sugar Syrup

Coring an apple is nearly impossible without the right tools. This recipe produces the same flavors as baked apples without all the work.

> **2 medium apples, peeled and quartered**
> **(without seeds)**
> **¼ cup brown sugar**
> **¼ cup water**
> **cinnamon**
> **vanilla ice cream, ice milk, frozen yogurt**
> **or whipped cream, optional**

Place the apples in a baking pan. Boil the brown sugar and the water in a microwave safe bowl for about one minute, until the brown sugar dissolves in the water. Pour this over the apple slices. Sprinkle cinnamon over the apples slices. Carefully place in a 350° oven. Bake 20-30 minutes, depending on how big your apples are. Serve warm, with ice cream, if desired.

Sautéed Apple Slices

> **1 apple, sliced**
> **1 tablespoon butter**
> **1 tablespoon sugar**
> **¼ teaspoon cinnamon**

In a sauté pan, melt the butter. Sauté the apples. Stir in the sugar and cinnamon. Serve over waffles or pancakes.

Sticky Apple Coffeecake

> **2½ cups flour**
> **½ cup sugar**
> **1 package quick-rising yeast**
> **2 teaspoons cinnamon**
> **¼ cup olive oil**
> **1 cup skim milk, warmed**
> **2 eggs, beaten**

Topping

> **½ cup pecans**
> **¾ cup brown sugar**
> **¼ cup butter**
> **2 large apples, peeled and sliced**

Stir together dry ingredients. Mix in wet ingredients to form a sticky dough. Let rise until double, about 30 minutes. In a microwave safe bowl, microwave the butter and brown sugar for 30-40 seconds, stirring frequently, until bubbly.

In the bottom of a 9 inch square pan, pour the bubbly mixture. Then arrange the pecans and apples slices. Spread the dough over the topping. Let rise about ten minutes. Bake in a 350° F oven for 35-40 minutes until golden and the bread sounds hollow when tapped. Cool for five minutes. Remove coffeecake from the pan by covering the pan with a platter and flipping the whole thing over. Remove the pan and serve warm.

Easy Apple Cake

2 apples, peeled and sliced
½ cup sugar
2 teaspoons cinnamon
one yellow cake mix, prepared according to the
   box, minus the oil
½ cup applesauce

Toss the apples in the cinnamon and sugar. Prepare the cake mix according to the directions on the box, substituting the applesauce for the oil. Pour the cake into a prepared 9x13 inch pan. Layer the apples on top. Bake according to package directions, about 30 minutes.

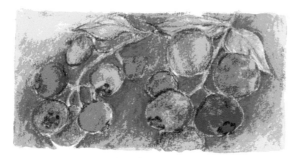

Blueberries

The University of Minnesota tests and develops different varieties and updates their Extension service website ***www.extension.umn.edu*** with the latest information. Some varieties they recommend include North-Blue, North-Country, North-Sky, St. Cloud, Polaris, and Chippewa. Grow two blueberry varieties for best pollination.

Planting: Blueberries need acidic soil (pH 4.0-5.0). Test your soil. If you need to change the pH, add amendments (peat moss is an organic choice), and test again.

Dig a hole 50 percent larger than the plant. Refill the hole with some of the loose soil, add the plant, and then return the rest of the soil, watering and firmly pressing the soil down. Add mulch to protect the plant and keep it moist.

Thinning: Pruning may be necessary for healthy plants. Cut away any dead branches. You may thin the blossoms for larger berries.

Harvesting: After the berries turn blue, wait a few days until they are sweet. Try to get them before the birds do, gently picking the berries.

Storing: If you have any blueberries left, they may be frozen. Place them on a cookie sheet to freeze, and then pour the frozen berries into an airtight container. Use frozen berries in recipes (they get mushy when thawed).

Helpful Hint: Birds love the fruit in the summer and rabbits love the bush in the winter. Protect the fruit with netting, and protect the bush with a wire fence. I've covered my bushes with burlap in the fall, which, along with lots of snow, tends to discourage the pests.

A Healthy Dose: Fifty blueberries have 38 calories and 1.8 grams of fiber as well as 60 milligrams of potassium.

Historical Notes: Blueberries are native to North America. Canned blueberries were used to feed Union soldiers during the Civil War.

Recipes

Blueberry Sauce

> **3 cups blueberries, washed, dried, and**
> **divided**
> **½ cup sugar**
> **1 tablespoon corn starch**

In a small saucepan cook all the ingredients except 1 cup blueberries over medium heat, stirring constantly, until it boils and thickens. Remove from the heat. Stir in the last cup of berries. Serve with cake, ice cream or cheesecake.

Cool Blueberry Pie

> **1 prepared cookie pie crust**
> **1 package cheesecake flavored instant pudding**
> **1 cup milk**
> **½ teaspoon almond extract**
> **1 8-oz tub frozen whipped topping**
> **1 recipe blueberry sauce, cooled completely**
> **¼ cup slivered almonds**
> **fresh blueberries for garnish, optional**

Mix together the instant pudding, milk, and extract. Stir in one cup of frozen whipped topping. Spread into the pie crust. Spread the blueberry sauce on top. Cover the pie with the rest of the frozen whipped topping. Arrange the blueberries and almonds on top. Serves 8.

Note: You may substitute whipped cream for the frozen whipped topping.

Mom's Blueberry Coffee Cake

Mom serves this when we visit and it never lasts very long.

> **¾ cup sugar**
> **¼ cup butter or margarine**
> **1 egg**
> **¾ cup milk**
> **2 cups flour**
> **2 teaspoons baking powder**
> **¼ teaspoon salt**
> **3 cups blueberries**

Topping

> **½ cup brown sugar**
> **¼ cup flour**
> **1 teaspoon cinnamon**
> **¼ cup butter or margarine**

Coat a 9-inch pan with vegetable oil spray. In a bowl, combine sugar, butter, and egg. Add milk. Stir in flour, baking powder, and salt. Gently fold in blueberries. Pour into the prepared pan. In another bowl, combine the topping ingredients until crumbly. Sprinkle the topping over the batter. Bake in a 350° F oven for 50 minutes, or until a toothpick inserted in the center comes out clean (not sticky with dough, though it may be stained with blueberry juice). Serving suggestion: serve warm with whipped cream. Serves 8.

Blueberry Banana Bread

1 box banana bread mix
2 cups blueberries
1 tablespoon flour

Prepare the mix according to package directions. In a bowl, toss the blueberries with the flour gently. Stir the blueberries in the mix. Bake as directed.

Note: You may use your favorite banana bread recipe in place of the mix.

Cherries

Minnesotans in central and southern Minnesota can grow sour cherries. Mesabi, Meteor, and Northstar are three varieties tested by the U of M Extension Service. Nanking (or Hansen bush) cherries should grow throughout the state. I just planted a Bali cherry tree, which grows to only ten feet.

Planting: Like apple trees, cherry trees need attention: pruning, spraying for insects and diseases during the season (organic products are available), and protecting the tree during the winter. Each winter I wrap all my fruit tree trunks.

Cherries need good drainage. Plant each tree or bush following the specific instructions from the nursery: Dig a large hole, mounding loose soil on the bottom, placing the tree carefully in the hole, and filling loose soil around the tree, watering carefully. Plant trees 25 feet apart, though dwarf varieties can be closer.

Harvesting: Taste before harvesting since cherries do not continue ripening once picked. Pull the cherry and stem carefully from the tree or bush, not injuring the spur.

Preparing: Tart cherries are good in many recipes. Do not eat the pits, which contain small amounts of cyanide.

Storing: Cherries may be stored in the refrigerator, but they don't last very long. For freezing, pit and then freeze the cherries in pre-measured amounts for your favorite recipe. Cherries can also be canned.

Helpful Hint: When the fruit begins to ripen, cover the trees with bird netting.

A Healthy Dose: One cup of pitted sour cherries has 78 calories and 2.4 grams of fiber as well as 25 milligrams of calcium and 1989 IU of vitamin A.

Historical Notes: Cherries, which are now grown around the world, may have originated in Asia Minor.

Recipes

Cherry Sauce with Almonds

This is great on ice cream or with the following recipe.

> **2 cups cherries, pitted**
> **1 tablespoon corn starch**
> **½ cup sugar**
> **1-2 tablespoons water**
> **¼ teaspoon almond extract**
> **¼ teaspoon orange extract**
> **¼ cup slivered almonds, toasted**

In saucepan, stir together sugar and corn starch. Add water and cherries. Stir over medium low heat until the sauce is slightly thickened. Remove from heat and add the extracts. Serve over ice cream and sprinkle with almonds.

Angel Food Cake with Cherry Sauce and Lemon Cream

> **1 angel food cake**
> **1 recipe cherry sauce with almonds**
> **½ can sweetened condensed non-fat milk**
> **16 oz light frozen whipped topping**
> **1 lemon (juice and zest)**

To make the lemon cream, mix milk, juice and zest and fold into the whipped topping. Slice the cake. Add a spoonful of cherry sauce and a spoonful of lemon cream to each slice. Sprinkle with the almonds and serve. Refrigerate any leftovers.

Sour Cherry Scones

In this recipe I've replaced the butter with canola oil to make a healthier scone.

> **2 cups flour**
> **1 cup cherries, pitted and chopped**
> **3 teaspoons baking powder**
> **½ teaspoon nutmeg**
> **¼ cup canola oil**
> **½ cup milk**
> **½ tablespoon honey**

Stir together baking powder and flour. Whisk together milk, oil, and honey, and add the mixture, along with the cherries, to the flour to make a sticky dough. Drop by spoonfuls onto a greased cookie sheet. Bake in a pre-heated 400° oven 12-15 minutes until lightly browned. Makes 12.

Ryan's Favorite Cherry Coffee Cake

> **1 cup sugar**
> **4 eggs**
> **1 cup applesauce**
> **2 cups flour**
> **1 teaspoon baking powder**
> **2 teaspoon salt**
> **1 recipe cherry sauce (without the almonds)**

Mix the sugar, eggs, and applesauce. Stir in the flour, baking powder, and salt. Spread ½ of the mixture in a 13x9 pan. Spread the cherry sauce evenly on top and then the remaining batter over that. Sprinkle with cinnamon and sugar. Bake 45-50 minutes in a preheated 350° oven. If desired, serve warm with ice cream or whipped cream.

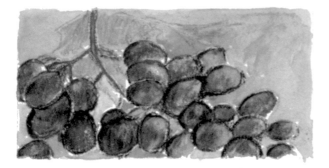

Grapes

The University of Minnesota Extension Service recommends extra protection in the winter for most grape varieties in Minnesota. For northern Minnesota, try Beta, Edelweiss and Valiant. For central and southern Minnesota, Bluebell, Fredonia, Swenson, and Worden should also grow. Concord and seedless grapes (Candice and Himrod) do best with extra winter protection, and then only in south-eastern Minnesota.

Planting: Plant grapes in full sun, preferably on a southern slope. Dig a hole deep enough so that the roots are not crowded. Grapes need well-drained soil. Grapes can be trained to grow on trellises.

Harvesting: Grapes may look ripe, but taste them before picking since they won't ripen off the vine.

Preparing: Beta, Bluebell, Concord, Valiant and Worden are good for juice and jelly making. Edelweiss is good for wine. All the recommended varieties but Beta are good for fresh eating.

Storing: Store grapes in the refrigerator after picking.

Helpful Hint: Avoid chemical herbicides, which can damage and even destroy grapes.

A Healthy Dose: One cup of grapes has 61 calories and one gram of fiber as well as 13 milligrams of calcium and 175 milligrams of potassium.

Historical Notes: The ancient Greeks loved grapes and especially the wine they made. Dionysus, the god of wine and wine-making, had a reputation for partying and trouble-making, though he had festivals in his honor.

Recipes

Grape Jelly

This is my grandmother's grape jelly recipe, interpreted from her notes in her cookbook.

Wash grapes, picking off the bad ones. Boil without water. Strain the juice. Add 3 cups of sugar to 2 cups juice and bring to a boil. Remove from the heat and stir for two minutes or until the sugar is dissolved. Pour into glass jars and seal.

Frozen Grapes

Freeze grapes in a single layer on a cookie sheet. Place in a sealed container when frozen. Serve frozen or partially thawed as these will be mushy when completely thawed. For fun, place a toothpick in a grape before freezing for instant grape Popsicles.

Ground Cherries

Ground cherries, also called husk tomatoes and cape gooseberries, are related to tomatillos but are often used like a cherry or berry in recipes. Some varieties include Pineapple Tomatillo, Golden Tomatillo, and Aunt Molly's.

Planting: Like tomatoes, it's best to use transplants. However, they will self-sow themselves and take over a patch of the garden if you let them. Plant them about 2 feet apart.

Harvesting: The fruit will turn a bright color when ready (red, or orange, depending on the variety) and the husk will be papery.

Preparing: Remove the husk before eating. The fruits can be eaten fresh.

Storing: These will store longer if left in the husk.

Helpful Hint: The fruits will fall from the plant when they are ripe.

A Healthy Dose: One cup of ground cherries has 74 calories as well as 15 milligrams of vitamin C and 1008 IU of vitamin A.

Melons

Cantaloupe (also known as muskmelon), honeydew, and watermelon are melons that can grow in Minnesota. Choose the early varieties, since we have such a short growing season here. The vines can easily take over a small garden, so try growing them up a trellis, or try a bush-type. For honeydew, try Earlidew. For cantaloupe, Athena, Earligold and Earlisweet, and Fastbreak should work in most areas of Minnesota.

Early maturing watermelons are often small but just as sweet than the big ones. Look for a bush or shorter-vined variety like Sugar Baby (six foot vines) for a small garden. New Queen ripens early and has a bright orange interior. Although it needs a longer growing season, the heirloom Moon and Stars watermelon has a green background with yellow "stars." Bitter melon (such as High Moon) is a "melon" native to southeast Asia, which is used for cooking and stuffing; it needs to be transplanted due to its later maturity.

Planting: Transplants are a better bet, but seeds can be grown in the garden (just hope for a warm spring or use row covers until the plants flower). Plant one transplant 2-4 feet apart, depending on the variety. For seeds, mound the dirt into a hill and plant 3-4 seeds. Place the mounds about 2-4 feet apart, depending on the variety.

Harvesting: When cantaloupe and honeydew easily come off the vine, then they are ready to be picked. Another hint is to smell the fruit; it should have a "ripe" fragrance. Ripe watermelons will be yellow (instead of white) on the bottom. Also, you can slap the palm of your hand to the fruit and listen for a hollow thud, though this could also indicate over-ripeness.

Storing: Store the fruit immediately in the fridge. They won't ripen on the counter. For longer storage, don't cut the melons.

Helpful Hint: As the growing season ends, pick the fruits that don't have a chance of ripening in time so the plant puts more energy into the already ripening ones.

A Healthy Dose: One cup of cubed cantaloupe has 56 calories and 1.2 grams of fiber as well as 67.5 milligrams of vitamin C and 5158 IU of vitamin A. One cup of diced watermelon has 48 calories and .7 gram of fiber as well as 14 milligrams of vitamin C.

Recipes

Any Fruit Salad

Cut bite-sized pieces of fruit and combine them together. This is a staple of our family get-togethers. Use whatever is in season: cantaloupe, red and green grapes, watermelon, blueberries, pitted cherries, etc. Drizzle with condensed milk, if desired.

Fruit Dip

7 oz. marshmallow crème
1 softened 4 oz package cream cheese

Stir together. Refrigerate.

Pears

Pears will grow best in southeastern Minnesota. The U of M Extension Service recommends Luscious, Parker and Pattern. Golden Spice, Gourmet, and Summercrisp should do fine in central Minnesota.

Planting: Plant two similarly maturing fruit trees for cross-pollination. Like apples trees, pear trees need attention:

pruning, spraying (organic products are available), and protecting the tree during the winter. Pears take longer to mature than apples trees.

Plant each tree following the specific instructions from the nursery: Dig a large hole, mounding loose soil on the bottom, placing the tree carefully in the hole, and filling loose soil around the tree, watering carefully. Plant trees 25 feet apart, though dwarf varieties can be closer.

Thinning: Thin the pears five to eight inches apart for larger fruits.

Harvesting: Pick carefully to avoid damaging the spur. Pick pears while they are still a bit green and allow them to ripen in a cool spot. Ripe fruits may be stored a short time in the refrigerator.

Preparing: Wash and eat.

Storing: For long term storage of pears, canning is recommended. Try freezing pears dipped in lemon juice for recipes. They will get too mushy for eating thawed.

Helpful Hint: Picking up fruits and leaves from the ground in the fall will help prevent disease and insect infestations the next year.

A Healthy Dose: One medium pear has 98 calories and 4 grams of fiber as well as 208 milligrams of potassium and 18 milligrams of calcium.

Recipes

Glowing Pears

Against the colored syrup, these pears seem to glow. Raspberry jam gives a reddish sauce, but try apricot for a golden sauce. Experiment for the best colors and flavors. Try substituting apples for the pears.

> **2 cups water**
> **¾ cup sugar**
> **¼ cup seedless raspberry jam (or other seedless jam or jelly)**
> **4 small pears, with stems but peeled**

Boil the water and the sugar together to dissolve the sugar. Stir in the jam. Slice a bit off the bottom of each pear. Place in a baking pan and pour the syrup over them. Bake in a preheated 375° F oven for 25-35 minutes until tender, basting often with the liquid. Check to see if they're done by carefully piercing with a small knife. Serve warm.

Pear Bars

> **¼ cup butter, softened**
> **¼ cup sugar**
> **1 cup unbleached flour**
> **1 large, firm pear**
> **1 tablespoon lemon juice**
> **¼ cup brown sugar**

Cream the butter and the sugar together. Mix in the flour. Press the mixture into the bottom of an eight inch square pan. Bake for ten minutes in a preheated 350° oven. Meanwhile, peel and slice the pear. Toss it with the lemon juice. Carefully stir in the brown sugar. When the crust is ready, arrange the slices and pour the sugary liquid over all the spaces. Bake in the oven for 12-15 minutes until the corners are golden brown and the brown sugar seems set (no "loose" juice).

Plums

Hybrid plums recommended by the U of M Extension Service for southern and central Minnesota include Alderman, LaCrescent, Pipestone, Redglow and Superior. All areas of Minnesota may grow South Dakota, Toka, and Underwood. European varieties for southeastern Minnesota include Mount Royal and Stanley.

Planting: Choose a protected place with good drainage and air circulation. Plant two similarly maturing hybrid plum trees for cross-pollination. European varieties are self-fruitful. Like apples trees, plum trees need attention: pruning, spraying (organic products are available), and protecting the tree during the winter.

Plant each tree following the specific instructions from the nursery: Dig a large hole, mounding loose soil on the bottom, placing the tree carefully in the hole, and filling loose soil around the tree, watering carefully. Plant trees 25 feet apart, though dwarf varieties can be closer.

Thinning: When the fruits are the size of marbles, thin them. Without thinning, the fruits will be quite small.

Harvesting: Harvest plums when they are soft, sweet, and in full color. Under-ripe plums will be sour.

Preparing: Just wash and eat these delicious fruits.

Storing: Fresh plums will keep in the refrigerator for a few days. Plums can be canned and dried. To freeze, remove the pit, and then dip the plum pieces in a store-bought ascorbic acid solution to preserve the color. Freeze in a container, measured for favorite recipes.

Helpful Hint: Pick plums slightly under-ripe for making jam.

A Healthy Dose: One plum has 36 calories and one gram of fiber as well as 114 milligrams of potassium and 213 IU of vitamin A.

Recipes

The Rice family gives my husband, a teacher, this jelly each fall. Delicious!

Plum Jelly

> **5½ cups plum juice**
> **1 package pectin (like Sure-Jel)**
> **7½ cups sugar**

Bring the juice and the pectin to a full boil for 1 minute. Add the sugar. Boil again for one minute. Pour into sterilized jars. Put on the canning lid and a screw cap. Flip the jars over for 5 minutes each to seal the jars.

Raspberries

Summer-bearing raspberries recommended by the U of M Extension Service include Latham, Boyne, Nordic, Festival, and Liberty. Brandywine is a purple variety recommended for all but northern Minnesota growers. Black raspberries (Bristol and Blackhawk) are recommended for southeastern Minnesota growers. Fall-bearing raspberry recommendations include Fall Red, Redwing, Summit, Autumn Bliss, and the yellow Fallgold. Ask a neighbor for a digging from their plant for an inexpensive way to try these berries.

Planting: Raspberries are tough to get rid of once planted, but why would anyone want to get rid of such a delicious treat? Dig holes, plant, and mulch thoroughly.

Thinning: Raspberries will spread. The older plants will be in the middle and can be cut back or dug out. Try giving some of the young ones to friends and neighbors.

Harvesting: Raspberries are ready when the fully colored fruit is easily plucked. These prickly plants can irritate your arms, so if you have a lot of picking to do, I suggest long sleeves or long gloves.

Storing: If you have any raspberries left, they may be frozen. Place them on a cookie sheet to freeze, and then pour the frozen berries into an airtight container. Use frozen berries in recipes (they get mushy when thawed).

Helpful Hint: Birds love raspberries. Protect the fruit with netting.

A Healthy Dose: One cup of raspberries has 60 calories and 8.3 grams of fiber as well as 27 milligrams of calcium and 30 milligrams of vitamin C.

Recipes

Very Berry Muffins

One package muffin mix
(such as cinnamon muffin mix)
One cup raspberries, washed and dried

Prepare the muffin mix according to package directions. Gently stir in the raspberries. Bake according to package directions, adding a minute or two. A toothpick inserted in the center should come out clean. Serves 6.

Note: You may substitute blueberries or sliced strawberries for the raspberries.

Any Fruit Shake

1 cup raspberries (or other fruit)
1 cup vanilla ice cream

Blend in a blender until smooth.

Note: Try different variations with the fruit and the frozen confection: blueberries with vanilla frozen yogurt, or strawberries and bananas with chocolate ice milk, raspberries with raspberry sherbet, etc.

Raspberry Pie

1 graham cracker pie shell
3 tablespoons sugar
1 tablespoon corn starch
2 cups fresh raspberries
1 4-oz package cream cheese, softened
⅓ cup sugar
½ cup whipping cream, whipped
fresh raspberries for garnish, optional

Combine the sugar and corn starch in a saucepan. Stir in the raspberries. Boil over medium heat for 2 minutes. Remove and cool about 15 minutes. Spread into the pie shell and refrigerate. Combine the sugar and cream cheese until fluffy. Fold in the whipped cream. Carefully spread over the raspberry filling. Cover and chill in the fridge. Garnish with fresh raspberries before serving. Serves 8.

Raspberry Walnut Bread

2 cups flour
1 cup sugar
1½ teaspoons baking powder
½ teaspoon baking soda
¼ cup margarine or butter
¼ cup sour cream
½ cup orange juice
1 teaspoon orange extract
1 egg, well beaten
½ cup chopped walnuts
3 cups raspberries

Sift together the dry ingredients. Cut in the margarine until the mixture is like coarse cornmeal. Combine the sour cream, orange juice and extract with the egg. Pour into the dry ingredients, mixing just until moistened. Fold in the nuts and raspberries. Pour into a 9x5 inch greased loaf pan, spreading the corners and sides higher than the center. Bake 350° for about 1 hour until the crust is golden brown and a toothpick inserted in the center comes out clean. Cool ten minutes. Remove from the pan.

Lisa's Petite Berry Trifles

1 large package vanilla pudding (or two small)
4 cups raspberries
1 loaf pound cake
1 cup seedless raspberry jam
½ 8 oz. tub frozen whipped topping
¼ cup sliced almonds

Prepare the pudding according to package directions. Chill. Slice the pound cake into 6 slices. Spread the jam on each slice. Place each slice, jam side up in 6 small bowls (clear glass bowls look pretty). Add ½ cup berries per bowl. Divide the pudding evenly and spread in each bowl. Add frozen whipped topping to each bowl. Sprinkle with almonds and the last remaining berries. Serves 6.

Note: Try using blueberries with blueberry jam, or strawberries with strawberry jam.

Rhubarb

This tasty tart treat tingles the taste buds! My rhubarb is a digging from my mother's plant. Many people share their rhubarb this way, but there are some nice varieties to try (Chipmans Canada Red and Valentine).

Planting: Rhubarb is best grown by division, but it can be planted from seed as well. Rhubarb likes fertile well-drained soil.

Harvesting: Use the stalks when they are tall yet young and tender. (Large stalks get tough and woody). Pull the stalks from the plant. Keep at least half the stalks so the plant can recover for the next year.

Storing: Chop and freeze rhubarb in recipe ready amounts in airtight containers.

Helpful Hint: Poison alert! Use only the stalk of the plant. Rhubarb leaves are poisonous, high in oxalic acid. Do not eat them or compost them.

A Healthy Dose: One cup of diced rhubarb has 25 calories and 2.2 grams of fiber as well as 104 milligrams of calcium.

Recipes

Spiced Rhubarb

This is my grandmother's recipe.

> **4 quarts rhubarb**
> **3 quarts sugar**
> **1 teaspoon vinegar**
> **1 pound raisins**
> **1 teaspoon allspice**
> **1 teaspoon cinnamon**
> **1 teaspoon cloves**

Cook until thick.

Rhubarb Sauce

> **3 cups chopped rhubarb**
> **1 cup sugar**
> **1 tablespoon corn starch**

In a small saucepan cook all the ingredients over medium heat, stirring constantly, until it boils and thickens. Serve with cake, ice cream or cheesecake.

Rhubarb Cherry Sauce with Crumb Topping

Sauce

> **4 cups chopped rhubarb**
> **1½ cups sugar**
> **¾ cup water**
> **3 tablespoons corn starch**
> **¼ cup water**
> **¼ teaspoon almond extract**
> **1 can cherry pie filling**

Cook the rhubarb, sugar and water in a saucepan until the rhubarb is soft. Mix 3 tablespoons corn starch with ¼ cup cold water. Stir into rhubarb mixture. Stir constantly until the mixture is thickened. Cool. Stir in the almond extract and pie filling. Serve with the topping. Serves 4.

Topping

> **1 cup oatmeal**
> **1 cup brown sugar**
> **1 cup flour**
> **1 cup butter**

Stir ingredients together. Sprinkle on a cookie sheet. Bake in a 350° F oven, stirring frequently.

Mary's Favorite Rhubarb Cream Torte

Crust

> **1 cup flour**
> **½ cup butter**
> **⅓ cup powdered sugar**
> **⅛ teaspoon salt**

Preheat oven to 375° F. Combine the ingredients with fingers until a dough is formed. Press evenly in the bottom of a 9 x 2½ inch springform pan. Bake 15 minutes.

Filling

> **1½ cup granulated sugar**
> **¼ cup flour**
> **2 large eggs, beaten**
> **½ teaspoon baking powder**
> **½ teaspoon vanilla extract**
> **3½ cups chopped fresh rhubarb**

While the crust is baking, mix the above ingredients. Spread the filling on the crust. Bake 45-50 minutes. Remove from the oven and cool 15 minutes. Run a wet, sharp knife between the pan and the torte; then remove the rim of the pan. Place the torte on a serving plate. Serve with ice cream, frozen yogurt, or whipped cream. Store in the fridge.Serves 8.

Rhubarb Orange Muffins

2 cups all purpose flour
½ cup sugar
1 teaspoon baking powder
1 teaspoon baking soda
½ teaspoon salt
2 eggs
½ cup butter, softened
½ cup orange juice
1 teaspoon orange extract
1½ cups chopped rhubarb

Orange Glaze
1 cup powdered sugar
1½-2 tablespoons orange juice

Sift together the dry ingredients. Beat the eggs with the butter, juice, and extract. Stir in the rhubarb. Mix in the dry ingredients just until moistened. Pour into a muffin tin lined with 12 paper muffin cups. Bake at 400° F for 20 minutes.

For the orange glaze, mix the powdered sugar with a little of the orange juice, adding orange juice until it's a drizzling consistency. Drizzle over the warm muffins. Serves 12.

Golden Rhubarb Pie

1 unbaked pie crust, placed in a pie pan
2 cups rhubarb cut into 1 inch pieces
1 cup sugar
2 eggs
1 tablespoon flour
2 tablespoons butter
rind of 1 orange
⅓ cup orange juice

Place the chopped rhubarb in the pie shell. Mix flour, sugar and butter. Separate eggs and beat the yolks. Add to flour mixture, and pour over rhubarb. Bake in a preheated 350° F oven for 35-45 minutes, until set in the center.

Meanwhile, to make the meringue, beat together the 2 egg whites with 4 tablespoons sugar, and ¼ teaspoon cream of tartar until peaks form. Spread it on the pie, and return it to the oven until brown.

Rhubarb Gelatin Jam

This recipe is a favorite passed among rhubarb lovers. Try strawberry, cherry, or raspberry for the gelatin.

5 cups rhubarb
3 cups sugar

Cut up rhubarb very fine. Add a little water and bring to a boil. Add the sugar and boil until mushy (very well done). Remove from heat and add one small box of any flavor gelatin. Stir until completely dissolved (this is important). Store in refrigerator.

Strawberries

Strawberries break down into three basic kinds: June-bearing (one big crop), ever-bearing (a spring and a smaller fall crop), and day neutral (constant crop). Pick varieties that advertise disease-resistance. If you are short on space, strawberries can be planted in pots! Some June bearing varieties are Crimson King and Lateglow. Everbearing and day neutral include Ft. Laramie, Ogallala, Tribute and Tristar. Ask neighbors for extra, unwanted plants and you're sure to get a variety that does well in your area.

Planting: Do not bury the crown. Plant in rows or on mounds. Mulch heavily to prevent disease and keep the plants moist. In the fall, keep a thick layer of mulch on the plants until they grow in the spring (they will start growing under the mulch, so pull it off quickly). Cover the plants with a row cover or cloth (not plastic) sheet if they are in danger of late spring frosts.

Thinning: Strawberry plants need to be renewed after a while, so keep the runner plants, while digging out the old plants in the fall.

Harvesting: The berries will be red... you can't miss 'em—although the wildlife in your neighborhood hopes you will. Gently pull the ripe berries from the plant. Clean up any berries than may have fallen to the grown to prevent disease.

Storing: If you have any strawberries left, they may be frozen. Place them on a cookie sheet to freeze, and then pour the frozen berries into an airtight container. Use frozen berries in recipes (they get mushy when thawed).

Helpful Hint: Birds and squirrels and chipmunks love strawberries. Protect the fruit with netting. And pick them quickly!

A Healthy Dose: One cup of strawberries has 43 calories and 3.3 grams of fiber as well as 81 milligram of vitamin C.

Historical Notes: Today's strawberries are derived from both the small native European varieties and the larger American ones.

Recipes

A summer tradition is picking berries at a berry farm. Even though it's a bit of work to pick and then clean the berries, the payoff is fresh and delicious.

Strawberry Sauce

3 cups clean, very ripe berries
1 cup powdered sugar
1 heaping tablespoon corn starch

In a large pot, mash the berries. Stir in the sugar and corn starch. Heat over medium heat until the mixture boils, and then thickens. Serve over cake, ice cream, or cheesecake.

Summer Dream Strawberry Pie

1 prepared graham cracker crust
1 package vanilla pudding, prepared according to pie directions
1 recipe strawberry sauce, chilled
4 cups strawberries, cleaned
sweetened whipped cream

Spread the prepared pudding in the pie crust. Chill. Place the strawberries on top of the pudding. Pour the sauce over the berries. Spread whipped cream over the top. Store in the refrigerator. Serves 8.

Sweetened Whipped Cream: Whip together ½ pint of heavy whipping cream, 2 tablespoons powdered sugar, and 1 teaspoon vanilla. Note: You may substitute frozen whipped topping for the whipped cream.

Strawberry Crisp

Try substituting whatever fruit is in abundance for the strawberries or perhaps different spices or flavorings for the almond extract.

4 cups strawberries
¼ cup sugar
2 tablespoons corn starch

Topping

¼ cup sugar
¼ cup flour
¾ cup oats
¼ cup butter, softened
½ teaspoon almond extract

Combine the berries, sugar, and corn starch. If your berries are especially juicy, add a bit more corn starch. Pour into a 9-inch pan. Combine the topping ingredients and spread over the berries. Bake in a 350°F oven for 30 minutes, until the top is golden.

Vegetables

For many gardeners, the food is why we garden, vegetables plucked from the garden minutes before serving. Barely cooked veggies from the garden are best, but sometimes we need a good recipe for variety (especially when the harvest is bountiful and … gasp…overwhelming).

Here are some easy suggestions for serving fruits and vegetables:

- sprinkle cooked veggies with crushed potato chips, Parmesan cheese, bacon bits, or seasoned bread crumbs

- dot hot veggies with butter and add a sprinkle of fresh herbs

- pour melted cheese over cooked veggies

- add chopped nuts

- stir-fry a mixture of veggies with a jarred stir-fry sauce

- add veggies to canned soups, boxed dinners (such as Hamburger Helper), or sauces (such as pasta sauce)

- marinate raw veggies with a store-bought vinaigrette dressing for an easy summer dish

- heat whatever veggies are abundant in canned broth, adding some thin spaghetti noodles for a quick soup

I experiment in the kitchen as I do in the garden. Sometimes the experiment works. Sometimes it doesn't. In any case I try to keep my sense of humor (as well as the phone number for the local pizza place).

A note about varieties: The varieties recommended in this book are currently offered in seed catalogs. Every year new varieties are offered, so look for the early maturing ones. Also, try heirloom vegetables, whose seeds can be saved year after year.

Asparagus

Asparagus is an early and exciting spring vegetable. Though it takes a bit of preparation and patience, asparagus is worth the wait. Jersey Giant and Jersey Knight will grow in Minnesota. Purple Passion is a purple variety. Mary Washington is a good choice in northern Minnesota.

Planting: Asparagus is a perennial vegetable; plant it once for several (perhaps up to 30) years of enjoyment. Prepare the asparagus bed well, adding lots of compost. Asparagus needs good drainage. Dig a trench, refill it six inches from the ground, place the asparagus crowns (roots) 18 inches apart in the trench and add a few inches of soil. As the crowns grow, fill the trench with soil up to ground level. Do not harvest any asparagus the first year. Lightly harvest year two, since it takes three years for the plants to establish themselves.

Harvesting: When the stalks are 8 inches, cut them at the ground (or just below). Pencil-thin asparagus will be tender and it gets woodier as it gets thicker. As the season progresses, leave some stalks to "fern," so the roots can store energy for the next season's crop.

Preparing: If the asparagus is a bit thick, peel the stem. Snap off the thick end if it's tough or woody. Steam asparagus standing upright with the tips pointing skywards so that the thicker, lower stems are cooked more than the thin tips. Or lay them flat in a skillet, adding a bit of water. Cook until the thickest part can be easily pierced with a knife. Overcooked asparagus will be mushy.

Storing: Asparagus can be stored in the refrigerator, but should be eaten as soon as possible.

Helpful Hint: Asparagus plants are male and female. The male plants produce many spears; the females produce larger spears and berries later in the season.

A Healthy Dose: One medium spear has 4 calories as well as 20 mcg of folate.

Historical Notes: The ancient Greeks thought that asparagus could cure toothaches, and the Romans enjoyed asparagus as a delicacy. Asparagus is a member of the lily family, just like leeks and onions.

Recipes

Parmesan Asparagus

> 1 pound asparagus
> ¼ cup butter
> ¼ cup parmesan

Melt the butter. Steam the asparagus. Place the warm asparagus on a serving platter. Pour the melted butter over the top. Sprinkle the parmesan on the asparagus. Serve hot.

Asparagus with Cashews

> 1 16-oz package bite-sized pasta
>   (such as mostaccioli)
> 2 tablespoons olive oil
> 1 large handful (1 pound) fresh asparagus,
>   cut into bite-sized pieces
> 1 yellow bell pepper, cut into bite-sized pieces
> 2 cloves of garlic, chopped
> pepper to taste
> ¼ cup fresh basil, chopped
> ¾ cup shredded Parmesan cheese, divided
> 1 cup cashew pieces

Prepare pasta. Set aside. Saute the asparagus and bell pepper in hot oil over medium heat until tender-crisp. Add the garlic, stirring occasionally, for 1 minute. Add black pepper and basil. Toss together hot pasta, asparagus mixture, ½ cup cheese, and cashews. Sprinkle servings with rest of cheese.

Spring Pasta Salad

1 cup bite-sized pieces of blanched and
** cooled asparagus**
1 cup blanched and cooled peas
1 tablespoon chopped parsley
1 box cooked and cooled pasta, such as penne
1 recipe oil and vinegar dressing
** (or a jar from the store)**
olives for garnish

Mix together and refrigerate until ready to serve.

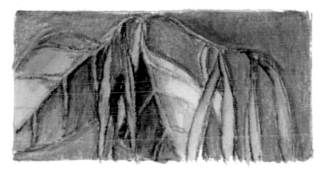

Beans

Green Beans: Pole bean varieties (Blue Lake and Kentucky Wonder) need a pole to grow up and up and up, while bush beans often don't need staking (though staking helps keep the beans off the ground). Romano is an Italian green bean with a flat pod. For a yellow bean, try Brittle Wax. For purple, try Royal Burgundy. Painted Lady runner beans are pretty as an ornamental; they grow tall like a pole bean, with pretty red and white flowers (and edible beans, too).

Dried Beans: Kentucky Wonder can be grown for its dried beans as well as the pods. Minnesotans can also grow the most popular dried bean varieties: Great Northern, Navy, Pinto, and Red Kidney.

Soybeans: Sayamusume is an edible soybean (edamame) that matures in 75 days. Check other varieties for early maturing dates since soybeans do not like cool soil.

Planting: Wait until the soil is warm (65 degrees F or more) to plant beans. Plant them one inch deep in the soil, two to three inches apart, after the last frost day. Plant extra rows in two week intervals for harvests throughout the season.

Thinning: Thinning beans is important because without air circulation, they are prone to disease. I got fewer beans when I had crowded plants too closely together. Space 8–12 inches between plants, depending on the variety.

Harvesting

Green Beans: A lot of the beans I harvest never make it into the house; they are so good sun-warmed and fresh. For tender beans, harvest them when they are the thickness of a pencil. Pull the mature bean off the plant, taking care not to pull off other pieces of the vine.

Dried Beans: The beans can be eaten after they are fully developed in the pod yet still soft, or left on the plant to dry. Pull the plant up and let the beans continue drying in a cool, dry place. Shell the beans, and store them once fully dried.

Soybeans: Once the beans in the pod are visible, pick the light green pods.

Preparing

Green Beans: Rinse and steam the beans until tender-crisp. I often add the tiniest bit of olive oil with a few snips of oregano. Green beans are also tasty served whole with a sprinkle of sliced almonds. Purple varieties turn green after they have been cooked.

Dried beans: Mark Bittman, in *How to Cook Everything*, dispels some bean myths.Beans do not need to be soaked before cooking; adding salt during the cooking process does not stop the beans from becoming tender; acid (lemon juice, vinegar) added during cooking will keep bean skins intact, and alkaline (baking soda) added during cooking will help the skins break down.

To cook beans, look over and rinse the beans. Bring a pot of water and beans to a boil. Reduce the heat and simmer, loosely covered. Cook until the beans are tender.

Soybeans: Bring a pot of salted water to a boil. Place the pods in the water and cook for three minutes. Rinse with cool water. Sprinkle with salt. Using fingers or teeth, eat the beans out of the pods.

Refrigerating

Store in covered container in the fridge for a few days.

Freezing

Green Beans: Boil whole beans or pieces in water for three minutes. Cool immediately in ice water. Drain completely and freeze, storing in an airtight container.

Dried Beans: Cooked beans can be frozen in their liquid.

Helpful Hint: Harvest beans when the plants are dry; diseases can be spread while the plants are damp from rain or dew.

A Healthy Dose: One cup of green beans has 34 calories and 2 grams of fiber as well as 40 milligrams of calcium and 40 mcg of folic acid.

Historical Notes: Soybeans have been popular in Japan and are now making way into American culture. Soybeans were first grown in America as an industrial product, but now the FDA suggests that eating soy may prevent heart disease and prostate cancer. The Aztecs ate corn tortillas with their beans. In the 1500s, the American scarlet runner bean appeared in English gardens.

Recipes

Green Bean Casserole

1 cup chopped tomatoes
½ cup orange juice
2 chopped cloves of garlic
½ cup thinly sliced onions
3 cups green beans
1 tablespoon fresh oregano
salt and pepper to taste
¼ cup bread crumbs

Combine all the ingredients except for the bread crumbs. Bake in a covered casserole dish for one hour. Stir. Top with ¼ cup bread crumbs, and bake, uncovered for 10-15 minutes, until the beans are tender and the crumbs are lightly browned. Serves 6.
    Note: Add other fresh or dried herbs if you like.

Cold Green Bean Salad

3 cups whole green beans, trimmed
½ cup thinly sliced red onion
½ cup yellow bell pepper, sliced into thin strips
2 tablespoons seasoned rice vinegar

Blanch the green beans (Place green beans in boiling water for one minute; remove them and place them in iced water; drain.) Combine the ingredients. Chill at least one hour in the fridge. Serves 6.
    Note: Use yellow beans with green peppers, or any bean and pepper combination to make a colorful salad.

Green Bean Stir Fry

3 cups green beans
1 inch fresh ginger, sliced
1 tablespoon olive oil
1 tablespoon soy sauce
1 cup thinly sliced carrots
1 8 oz can water chestnuts, drained

Stir fry all the ingredients until tender-crisp. Serves 4. Serve with noodles or rice.
    Note: Substitute other vegetables, if desired.

Italian Chicken Soup

1 tablespoon olive oil
1 onion, chopped
2 cloves garlic, chopped
2 cups chicken broth
2 cups puréed tomatoes
1 cup green beans
1 cup sliced carrots
1 green pepper, chopped
1 cup cooked chicken, shredded
2 cups cooked pasta (rotini works well)
1 tablespoon fresh oregano, chopped
¼ cup fresh basil, chopped

In a soup pot, cook the onion in the oil until tender. Add the rest of the ingredients, except the basil. Cook until the vegetables are tender. Add the basil and cook for about one minute. Serves 4.

Oregano Green Beans

2 cups green beans
1 tablespoon oregano
1 teaspoon olive oil

Steam green beans. Add oregano and oil. Serve hot.

Chili

Everyone has their favorite chili recipe and this one is mine. I adjust the hot pepper content according to who will eat it. With all these great flavors, I never need to add salt.

1 tablespoon olive oil
1 pound ground turkey
1 onion chopped
4 garlic cloves, finely chopped
2 jalapeño peppers, chopped
5 tomatoes, chopped
2 cups red beans, already cooked
1 tablespoon cocoa powder
freshly ground black pepper, to taste
1 tablespoon fresh oregano
tomato paste, optional
1 sweet green pepper, chopped

Brown the ground turkey in the olive oil. Add the onions and cook until they are translucent. Add the garlic and cook for another minute. Add the jalapeños, tomatoes and beans. Stir in the cocoa, the black pepper, and the oregano. Simmer. If your tomatoes are juicy and the chili is too thin, add tomato paste to thicken it. Just before serving, add the chopped green pepper and simmer until it's tender.

Refried Bean Soup

This is Arlene's favorite bean soup recipe.

1 tablespoon olive oil
2 cups chopped onion
2 cups chopped green pepper
1 clove chopped garlic
1 can (14 oz) fat-free chicken broth
2 cups chopped tomatoes
1½ cups black beans
1½ cups red kidney beans
1 medium can fat-free refried beans
black pepper

Saute onion, garlic, and pepper in oil until tender. Add garlic, broth, and tomatoes and stir. Add the beans and re-fried beans. Stir well and let mixture come to a boil, reduce heat and simmer for 15 minutes. Season with black pepper to taste.

See Also
Cabbage: Minestrone
Radishes: Radishes and Black Beans on Rice

Beets

Some people think red beets are too much trouble because of how much they stain, but there are gold (Golden) and white (Albina Verdura) varieties as well. Red Ace is a red, round beet; Cylindra, an oblong beet, grows up to 8 inches long. Chiogga, an heirloom red and white ringed variety, is pretty as well as extra sweet.

Planting: Beets can be planted in cool weather. As with any root vegetable, make sure the soil is loose and rock-free. Add lots of compost.

Thinning: Try thinning beets by clipping the greens with a scissors to avoid disturbing the roots. Beet greens can be eaten…ask any bunny how good they are. Thin to 4 inches (or more, depending on how large the variety will grow) between plants.

Harvesting: Check the variety when you plant. Some can stay in the ground and grow quite large without hampering their quality; others can't. Using a pitchfork or shovel, loosen the soil around the beet and gently pull it from its spot.

Preparing: Slice off the tops and bottoms of the beets. Boil beets for about 50 minutes (until tender). Slip off the skin (carefully—they're hot). Then slice and eat. Also, julienne (slice into match-stick shapes) roasted beets for adding to salads.

Storing: Store beets in the fridge or try pickling them.

Helpful Hint: Pick every other beet early for baby beets, allowing the remaining to grow larger.

A Healthy Dose: One half cup of cooked and drained beets has 37 calories and 1.7 grams of fiber as well as 68 mcg of folic acid.

Historical Notes: Romans originally used beet roots medicinally and only later cooked them.

Recipe

Grandma Dell's Beet Pickles

This recipe belonged to my father-in-law's mother, beloved by the whole family. I include it for a bit of nostalgia as well as something to do if you have too many beets.

> **6 quart jars filled with cooked, peeled,
>   and cut beets**
> **5 cups vinegar**
> **4 cups sugar**
> **2 cups water**
> **1 small bag of pickling spice**
> **6 teaspoons salt, separated**
> **6 - 12 cinnamon sticks**

Boil together the vinegar, sugar, and water. Add the spice bag. Remove spice bag and carefully pour the hot liquid over the beets in the jars.

Add 1 teaspoon salt and a cinnamon stick or two to each quart. Seal the jars.

Vegetable Borscht

When I asked my friends for another beet recipe, Kirsten came to the rescue!

> 1 tablespoon olive oil
> 1 onion, chopped
> 2 large fresh beets: remove, wash and chop
>   the greens; cook, peel, and chop the root
> 1 medium carrot, sliced
> 1 large potato, peeled and cubed
> 4 cups vegetable broth
> ½ small head cabbage, shredded
> 2 large tomatoes, chopped
> 2 tablespoons fresh parsley
> 1 tablespoon fresh dill
> freshly ground pepper
> lemon juice
> optional: sour cream for garnish

In a large saucepan, cook the onions until tender. Add the carrot, potato, and stock. Simmer for 20 minutes, skimming foam if necessary. Add the beet greens, cabbage, tomato, parsley, and dill. Simmer for 10 minutes longer. Add the chopped beet roots and simmer until they are heated through and all the vegetables are tender. Season with pepper and lemon juice to taste. Add a bit of sour cream to each bowl. Serves 8.

Broccoli

The store bought version cannot compare to broccoli out of the garden. I recommend buying broccoli plants from your local nursery rather than growing them from seed, since we have a short growing season here. Seeds could be started indoors (or under a cold-frame) by the adventurous gardener. Varieties that work well in Minnesota include Bonanza, Green Comet, Packman, and Small Miracle (a compact plant). Broccoli Raab is not officially broccoli, though it is used just as broccoli is.

Planting: Place broccoli plants 2 feet apart, mulching to prevent weeds. Broccoli prefers cool weather, so it will flower quickly once the weather gets hot. Broccoli can be planted in the middle of the growing season for a fall harvest.

Harvesting: Harvest when the "head" has tight green buds. Later these buds will produce yellow flowers, which are also edible. Do not cut the whole plant down. With a sharp knife, cut the "head" of the broccoli off the stalk, leaving the base and leaves. The plant will put out smaller shoots to eat later.

Preparing: Rinse the broccoli well, cut into bite-sized pieces, and steam just until bright green.

Storing: Keep in a covered container in the fridge for a few days. For freezing, cut into pieces, boil in water for three minutes, plunge into ice-cold water, drain well, and freeze in an air-tight container.

Helpful Hint: Submerge broccoli in cold, salty water immediately before cooking. This way, the tiny green worms that like to eat the broccoli will be forced out.

A Healthy Dose: One cup of chopped broccoli has 24 calories and 2.6 grams of fiber as well as 42 milligrams of calcium and 82 milligrams of vitamin C.

Historical Notes: Broccoli is an Italian vegetable, which didn't become popular in the United States until 1927, with the help of Italian American farmers.

Recipes

Broccoli Soup

> **4 cups chicken broth**
> **2 cloves garlic, chopped**
> **8 oz angel hair pasta**
> **1 tablespoon chopped basil**
> **2 cups broccoli, cut into bite-sized pieces**

Bring the broth and garlic to a boil in a large pot and add the angel hair pasta. Simmer until the pasta is done. Add the broccoli and basil and simmer for 1 minute. Serves 4.

Note: For a heartier soup, add one cup cooked chicken.

Summer Pasta Salad

> **1 cup broccoli, cut into bite-sized pieces**
> **1 cup cauliflower, cut into bite-sized pieces**
> **1 cup carrots, cut into bite-sized rounds**
> **1 cup cherry tomatoes**
> **1 1lb. box tri-color rotini**
> **1 16 oz. bottle of (spicy) Italian salad dressing**
> **sliced black olives (optional)**

Cook the pasta, subtracting 1–2 minutes from the recommended cooking time. Rinse with cold water and drain. Toss the pasta, the vegetables, and ½ the bottle of dressing. Refrigerate at least one hour. Before serving, add more salad dressing, if desired. Serves 8.

Note: Personally, I like less salad dressing so I can taste the veggies and then the pasta doesn't get too soggy. This recipe can be made the night before and doubles easily for those huge family picnics. Add green beans, radishes, or other veggies for variety. Experiment with vinaigrettes or reduced fat dressings as well (though non fat dressings don't seem to work as well).

Parmesan Broccoli

> **1 cup cooked broccoli**
> **1 tablespoon shredded Parmesan cheese**

Sprinkle warm broccoli with Parmesan cheese. Serves 2.

Pasta and Broccoli Bake

4 cups broccoli, cut into bite-sized pieces
1 lb pasta (mostaccioli works well)
1 26-ounce jar of pasta sauce or the easy marinara
(recipe in the tomatoes section)
1 8-oz bag of shredded mozzarella cheese

Cook a pound of pasta according to package directions, adding the broccoli for the last 30 seconds of cooking. Drain the pasta and broccoli. Stir in the pasta sauce. Pour into a greased 9 x 13 inch pan. Top with cheese. Bake, covered, in a 350 degree oven for 20 minutes. Uncover and bake an additional 5-10 minutes. Serves 6.

Note: Feel free to add other vegetables such as carrots or cauliflower.

See Also

Cabbage: Vegetable Slaw
Cauliflower: Baked Cauliflower and Broccoli
Potatoes: Twice Baked Potatoes

Brussels Sprouts

Brussels sprouts are related to cabbage and broccoli and like cooler weather. Jade Cross (for its abundant yield), Prince Marvel (for its flavor) and Bubbles (for its tolerance to warm weather) are three varieties to try.

Planting: Use transplants for best results. They will need fertilization (organic fertilizer or an application of compost) every two weeks for best production. Try planting in mid-season for a fall harvest.

Harvesting: When the sprouts are one inch in diameter, cut them off with a sharp knife, leaving the rest of the plant intact for an extended harvest.

Storing: Brussels sprouts will keep in the refrigerator for 3 or 4 weeks.

Preparing: Steam or boil the sprouts just until tender, about 10 minutes, being careful not to overcook.

Helpful Hint: The flavor of Brussels sprouts is best after a frost.

A Healthy Dose: One sprout has 8 calories and just under a gram of fiber as well as 8 milligrams of calcium and 16 milligrams of vitamin C.

Historical Notes: Aptly named Brussels sprouts were developed in Belgium.

Recipes

Substitute Brussels spouts for the asparagus in Parmesan Asparagus, or try just about any sauce for vegetables.

Brussels Sprouts Soup

Substitute just about any root vegetable in this recipe.

> 1 tablespoon olive oil
> 1 onion, finely chopped
> 1 carrot, finely chopped
> 1 stalk of celery, finely chopped
> 1 potato, cut into bite-sized pieces
> 1 sweet potato, cut into bite-sized pieces
> 1 parsnip, finely chopped
> 1½ cups Brussels sprouts, halved
> 3 cups chicken broth
> 1 sweet red pepper, cut into bite-sized pieces
> black pepper to taste
> ½ cup chopped basil (or dill or parsley)

Cook the onion in the olive oil until translucent. Add the carrot, celery, potatoes, parsnip, the Brussels sprouts, black pepper, and chicken broth. Simmer until the vegetables are tender. Add the red pepper and simmer until tender-crisp. Before serving, add the basil.

Cheese Sauce for Vegetables

> 1 tablespoon olive oil
> 1 tablespoon flour
> ½ cup milk
> 1 cup shredded cheese
> (reduced fat sharp cheddar works well)

Warm the olive oil over medium heat. Whisk in the flour and cook until the flour begins to brown, about three minutes. Be sure to cook the flour otherwise the sauce tastes like paste. Slowly stir in the milk. Cook until the milk thickens and then stir in the cheese. Serve warm over warm veggies.

See Also
Rutabaga: New England Boiled Dinner

Cabbage

Cabbage comes in green and red, early and late varieties, the late ones being a bit more tolerant of being left in the garden at maturity. Try early Stonehead, red Sombrero, or late Savoy Ace.

Planting: Transplants are best, planting them about 18 inches apart. Cabbage needs even moisture and lots of organic matter for fertilizer.

Harvesting: As soon as the heads are full, harvest immediately as the heads can split or burst open. Cut the head from the stem.

Storing: Store in the fridge. Cabbage keeps very well in a cool place.

Preparing: Peel off the outer leaves and cut out the core. Cabbage is good raw in salads as well as stir-fried. One easy way to cook cabbage is to blanch it in boiling water for two minutes, which turns it a bright color and doesn't make it mushy.

Historical Notes: Cabbage originated from sea cabbages growing on European coasts.

Helpful Hint: Leave a few leaves on the cabbage when harvesting to protect the head.

A Healthy Dose: One cup of shredded cabbage has 17.5 calories and 1.6 grams of fiber as well as 32 milligrams calcium.

Recipes

Super Simple Cabbage Salad

> 1 quarter small cabbage, shredded
> 1 teaspoon seasoned rice vinegar
> dash pepper

Toss together. Chill. Serves 2.

Minestrone

> 1 tablespoon olive oil
> 3 carrots, chopped
> 3 stalks celery, chopped
> 1 onion, chopped
> 2 cloves garlic, chopped
> 4 large tomatoes, chopped
> 1 zucchini, chopped
> 4 cups beef broth
> 1 15-oz can great northern beans
> 2 cups shredded cabbage
> shredded Parmesan cheese, optional

Cook carrots, celery, and onion in the oil for about 3 minutes. Add the garlic, tomatoes, zucchini, broth, and beans. Cook until tender, about 10 minutes. Add the shredded cabbage and cook for about 2 minutes. Serve with cheese sprinkled on top. Serves 4.

Cabbage Roll Hot Dish

> 1 cabbage
> 1 lb hamburger
> 1 small onion, finely chopped
> ½ teaspoon pepper
> ½ cup cooked rice
> 2 cups tomato sauce

Cook meat, onion, salt & pepper until crumbly. Place a layer of shredded cabbage on bottom of casserole dish. Mix hamburger & rice together and spread evenly on shredded cabbage. Place another layer of cabbage on top of hamburger. Dilute the tomato sauce with a little water and pour it over cabbage. Bake in 350° F oven about 30 minutes, until heated through. Serves 4.

Vegetable Slaw

Really, any vegetables can be chopped and added. Have fun with different combinations.

> ¼ cup mayonnaise
> ¼ cup sour cream
> 1 tablespoon white vinegar
> ¼ teaspoon black pepper
> 3 cups shredded cabbage
> 1 cup chopped carrots
> 1 cup chopped red pepper
> 1 cup fresh broccoli flowerets, chopped
> 1 cup fresh cauliflower flowerets, chopped
> ½ cup chopped purple onion
> 2 tablespoons parsley, chopped

Stir together first 5 ingredients in a large bowl. Stir in the veggies and parsley. Chill well before serving.

See Also
> Beets: Vegetable Borscht
> Rutabaga: New England Boiled Dinner

Carrots

I enjoy the Red Cored Chantenay, which sweetens as it cools, whether in the ground or in the fridge. It is a short, fat carrot good even for clay soils. Other good varieties include Nantes, for Northern Minnesota, and Nutri-Red, with the antioxidant lypocene. Sweet Sunshine is a yellow carrot.

Planting: For carrots and other root crops, be sure the soil is free of rocks and lumps, digging deeply to loosen the soil, so the carrots can grow straight and true. Carrot seeds are small, so scatter them carefully. Mix carrots with radishes to mark the rows and naturally thin the carrots. Or mix the tiny seeds with sand to thin them. With a hoe or small shovel, make a ¼-inch line in the soil, sprinkle the seeds down the line, and then pat the soil gently onto the seeds. Keep the soil moist for good germination. Plant in two-week intervals to extend the harvest. Note: Carrots like a little moisture; without it, they become woody. With too much, they rot.

Thinning: Carrots must be thinned. (Be ruthless; once I couldn't pull up my carrot seedlings, so I had lush, green plants, but no carrots.) Thin two to three inches between plants.

Harvesting: Check the variety for specific times. Look for fat crowns and fully colored roots. Carrots pulled too early may be small but edible. Carrots pulled too late will be tough and "hairy" (covered in tiny roots). Lower a pitchfork into the soil a few inches from the roots. Slowly lean on the fork until the roots are loosened and easily pulled from the ground.

Preparing: Rinse and eat fresh, or peel, slice into thin rounds, and steam until tender-crisp. Add butter, dill, or pepper, if you like.

Storing: Place in the fridge without the green tops in a plastic bag with tiny holes or slits for a couple weeks. To freeze, peel, slice into thick rounds, and boil for 3 minutes. Cool immediately in ice water. Drain completely and freeze.

Helpful Hint: Plant onions near carrots to repel carrot-loving insects.

A **Healthy Dose**: One cup of sliced carrots has 52 calories and 3.6 grams of fiber as well as 34317 IU of vitamin A.

Historical Notes: Carrots are probably descendants of the wild carrot, also know as Queen Anne's Lace.

Recipes

Saucy Carrots

> 1 tablespoon butter
> 1 teaspoon cornstarch
> 1 tablespoon brown sugar
> 2 tablespoons orange juice
> 1½- 2 cups of very thinly sliced carrots

In a skillet over medium heat, melt the butter. Stir in cornstarch, brown sugar and orange juice. Add the carrots. Heat, stirring constantly, until carrots are tender-crisp. Serves 2.

Note: This can be used with pre-cooked, sliced beets as well.

Easy Carrot Muffins

> 1 cinnamon muffin mix
> ½ cup shredded carrots
> ½ cup chopped walnuts

Follow the directions for the mix. Then add the carrots and nuts. Bake according to package directions, adding a minute or two. A toothpick inserted in the center should come out clean. 6 servings.

Carrot Stew

- 1 tablespoon olive oil
- 1 pound boneless beef sirloin, cut into bite-sized pieces
- 1 package onion soup mix
- 2 cups pureed tomatoes
- 2 cups water
- 2 cups sliced carrots
- 2 cups other vegetables (such as potatoes, onions, turnips, rutabagas, parsnips), cut into bite-sized pieces

Cook the meat in the oil until browned. Add the other ingredients, simmering until tender, about 10 minutes. Serves 4.

Carrot Cake, a. k. a. Everything But The Kitchen Sink Cake

This is delicious served warm and, with the abundance of flavors, doesn't need any frosting.

- 1½ cups sugar
- ½ cup canola oil
- ½ cup applesauce
- 3 eggs
- 1 teaspoon vanilla
- ½ teaspoon orange extract
- 2 cups flour
- 1 teaspoon cinnamon
- ¼ teaspoon nutmeg
- ¼ teaspoon ginger
- ⅛ teaspoon cloves
- 1 cup carrots, finely grated
- 1 cup crushed pineapple
- 1 cup shredded coconut
- ½ cup raisins
- ½ cup chopped pecans

Preheat the oven to 350° F. Spray a 9 x 13 inch pan with vegetable oil spray. Mix the sugar, oil, applesauce, eggs, and extracts until blended. Add the flour and spices. Stir in the final ingredients except for the nuts. Pour into the pan and sprinkle the top with the pecans. Bake for 30-35 minutes, until a toothpick inserted in the center comes out clean.

See Also
- Beans: Green Bean Stir Fry, Italian Chicken Soup
- Beets: Vegetable Borscht
- Broccoli: Summer Pasta Salad
- Brussels Sprout Soup
- Cabbage: Minestrone, Vegetable Slaw
- Cauliflower: Cauliflower and Carrot Soup
- Corn: Mexican Chicken Soup
- Parsnips: Roasted Parsnips and Carrots
- Potatoes: Potato Soup
- Rutabaga: New England Boiled Dinner
- Culinary Herbs: Ultimate Flu Fighting Chicken Noodle Soup
- Peanuts: Chicken Wraps

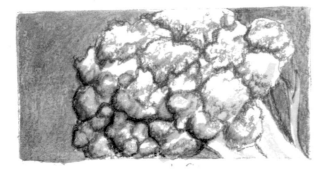

Cauliflower

The "self-blanching" cauliflower varieties are probably the variety offered at your local garden center, though the leaves can still be wrapped and tied so the cauliflower remains white, if perfection matters. Snow Crown is reliable and Early Dawn is extra early.

Planting: I recommend transplants, though seeds could be used. Plants should be about 18 inches apart.

Harvesting: The head will be compact, but just starting to separate. Cut the head from the stem.

Preparing: Rinse the cauliflower well, cut into bite-sized pieces, and steam just until tender. Season with butter and black pepper.

Storing: Keep in a covered container in the fridge for a few days. For freezing, cut into pieces, boil in water for three minutes, plunge into ice-cold water, drain well, and freeze in an air-tight container.

Helpful Hint: In order to be completely white, cauliflower tops need shade. Tie the outer leaves together when the cauliflower has started to form.

A Healthy Dose: One cup of cauliflower has 25 calories and 2.5 grams of fiber as well as 303 milligrams of potassium and 57 mcg of folic acid.

Historical Notes: Cauliflower originated in the Mediterranean and Asia Minor in the first century.

Recipes

Baked Cauliflower and Broccoli

> **2 cups broccoli, cut into bite-sized pieces**
> **2 cups cauliflower, cut into bite-sized pieces**
> **1 cup shredded Swiss cheese**

Spray a 9-inch baking pan with non-stick vegetable spray. Place the veggies in the pan and cover with the cheese. Bake in a 350° F oven for 8-10 minutes, until the cheese is melted. Serves 4.

Cauliflower and Broccoli Salad

> **2 cups broccoli, cut into bite-sized pieces**
> **2 cups cauliflower, cut into bite-sized pieces**
> **½ cup creamy Italian dressing**
> **sliced olives, optional**

Combine the veggies with the dressing. Sprinkle with the olives. Serves 4.

Cauliflower and Carrot Soup

> ½ onion, chopped
> 1 tablespoon olive oil
> 1 head of cauliflower, cut in pieces (about 4 cups)
> 6 carrots, peeled and sliced (about 2 cups)
> 2 cups water
> 3 cloves of garlic, peeled
> 1½ cups reduced fat Colby cheese
> 1 teaspoon black pepper

In a soup pot, cook the onion in the olive oil until translucent. Add the cauliflower, carrots, garlic, and water. Cover the pot and cook until the vegetables are tender and easily pierced with a fork, about 15 minutes. In a blender, puree the soup in small batches, taking care since it is hot. Return to the soup pot and re-heat, adding the cheese and the pepper. Serves 4.

Cauliflower Cheese Salad

> 1 head of cauliflower, cut in pieces (about 4 cups)
> 1 red onion, sliced
> 2 tablespoons olive oil
> 1 cup shredded cheddar cheese
> pepper to taste
> chopped chives

Blanch the cauliflower by placing the pieces in boiling water, remove and cool. Cook the onion in the olive oil until tender. Season with black pepper. Toss the cauliflower, onion, and cheese together. Sprinkle with chives and serve warm.

See Also
Broccoli: Summer Pasta Salad
Cabbage: Vegetable Slaw

Celery

Celery requires a long growing season. For supermarket-type stalks, try growing Ventura. For the leaves (which are used as flavoring), try growing cutting celery, which requires a shorter growing season.

Planting: Celery takes a lot of time so use transplants. Dig in a lot of compost before planting and fertilize (organic fertilizer or an application of compost) every two weeks. Water evenly throughout the season.

Harvesting: Single stalks can be removed as needed from the plants. At the end of the season, pull the entire plant and remove the roots for storing

Preparing: Celery is good raw. Simply rinse and munch. Chop for salads. If the stalks are getting thick and old, try "peeling" them so they are less chewy.

Storing: Wrapped celery will store in the refrigerator for a few weeks.

Helpful Hint: Celery needs temperatures above 55° F to do well.

A Healthy Dose: One medium stalk has 6 calories as well as 16 milligrams of calcium.

Historical Notes: Celery, whose leaves have been used for flavoring before the stalks were eaten for food, was originally used as medicine.

Recipes

Ants on a Log

This is a tricky way to get kids to eat celery. I never fell for it, eating only the "good" parts, but I like celery now so maybe it wasn't a complete waste. Cut the celery into three inch pieces. Fill the crevice with peanut butter. Add raisins on top.

Tuna Salad Sandwiches

As a kid, this was my brother's favorite sandwich. Only Mom knows the best way to make it!

> 1 can light tuna, drained
> 1 cup salad dressing or mayonnaise
> ¾ cup chopped celery
> 2 green onions, chopped
> 1 tablespoon skim milk

Mix together and spread on fresh bread.

Beef Stir Fry

> One pound thinly sliced round steak
> 2 tablespoons olive oil
> 2 stalks celery, sliced
> 2 medium green peppers, sliced into strips
> 1 large onion, sliced into strips
> 2 gloves garlic, finely chopped
> 1 ½ cups beef broth
> 1 tablespoon lite soy sauce
> 2 tablespoons corn starch
> ¼ cup water
> 4 cups cooked rice

Brown the meat in the olive oil. Add the celery, green peppers, and onion and stir-fry until tender. Add the garlic. Add the broth and soy sauce and heat to boiling. Stir the corn starch into the water, then add to the broth, stirring constantly. Once the sauce has thickened, serve over hot rice.

Blasted Veggie Soup

My creative child came up with the title for this recipe. The base for the soup is tasty alone, but even better with a variety of vegetables. If you find that you need to add more veggies, feel free to increase the amount of chicken broth.

> 2 tablespoons olive oil
> 2 onions, finely chopped
> 2 cups cooked Italian sausage
> 1 head of garlic, peeled and chopped
> 3 cups chicken broth
> 2 cups vegetables, cut into bite-sized pieces, such as carrots, celery, asparagus, beans, Jerusalem artichoke, okra, parsnips, peppers, potatoes, rutabagas, sweet potatoes, turnips, zucchini

Brown the onions and the sausage in the olive oil. Add the garlic and cook for about one minute. Add the broth and the vegetables you choose. Add the longer cooking veggies first (potatoes, for example) and the quick cooking veggies at the very end (peas and asparagus). Simmer until the vegetables are tender.

See Also

Brussels Sprouts: Brussels Sprouts Soup
Cabbage: Minestrone
Cucumber: Cucumber and Sweet Pepper Salad
Okra: Okra Stew
Potatoes: Traditional Potato Salad
Rutabaga: New England Boiled Dinner

Celeriac

This is the root version of celery and also needs a long growing season. Large Prague and Brilliant are two varieties to try.

Planting: Celeriac needs fertile soil, so add lots of compost before planting transplants.

Harvesting: The roots can be harvested when they are two inches in diameter or wait until the end of the season for a full sized vegetable.

Preparing: Peel, chop, and simmer until soft. Try mashing with potatoes.

Storing: Store in a cool, dry place.

Helpful Hint: Keep celeriac thickly mulched and evenly watered throughout the season.

A Healthy Dose: I cup of celeriac has 65 calories and 2.8 grams of fiber as well as 67 milligrams of calcium and 156 milligrams of sodium.

Recipes

Substitute celeriac for part of mashed potatoes or roasted root vegetables.

See Also

Brussels Sprouts: Brussels Sprout Soup
Carrots: Carrot Stew
Celery: Blasted Veggie Soup
Parsnips: Trish's Root Vegetable Chicken Soup
Rutabaga: Roasted Root Vegetables, New England Boiled Dinner

Corn

Sweet corn comes in yellow and white and also red (Ruby Queen). There's also blue corn (such as Hopi Blue Dent, for grinding) and ornamental corn (Mini-colored popcorn or Earthtones). Every seed catalog has abundant choices. Here is a sample of what the University of Minnesota Extension Service recommends for Minnesota gardeners—Sugar Enhanced (SE): Seneca Pronto (yellow), Quickie (bi-color), Alpine (white); Shrunken Super Sweets (Sh2): Northern Super Sweet, Early Extra Super Sweet (both recommended for Northern Minnesota); Pop Corn: Pretty Pops, Iopop 12.

Have fun choosing varieties, but try to make sure they mature early.

Planting: Plant seeds 1-2 inches deep, about 2 inches apart. Plant 4 rows by 4 rows for best pollination of the sweet corn plants. Also, plant different varieties (such as a different kind of sweet corn or popcorn) far away or at a two-week interval between maturation dates to avoid cross-pollination (which results in not-so-sweet corn).

Thinning: Thin to 8 inches between plants.

Harvesting: Remove the ears after the corn silk has turned dry and brown, and the kernels, when punctured, are milky.

Preparing: After removing the husks and silk, boil the ears until hot, about 10 minutes.

Storing: If you're not going to eat the ears immediately, store them in the fridge. Corn can also be frozen on the cob with the husks removed or the kernels sliced from the cobs

Helpful Hint: Plant squash (or cucumber or pumpkins) between the corn plants. Raccoons do not like to walk on the prickly vines. For added nitrogen, plant beans near the corn stalks, which will act as a trellis for the beans. Native American farmers developed this technique called "The Three Sisters."

A Healthy Dose: One ear of cooked corn has 83 calories and 2 grams of fiber as well as 35 mcg of folic acid and 167 IU of vitamin A.

Historical Notes: Corn, or maize, derives from a wild grass. It was domesticated in Mexico.

Recipes

Sweet Corn Soup

1 tablespoon olive oil
1 onion, chopped
2 cloves of garlic, chopped
2 large potatoes, cubed
2 cups sweet corn
1 14½ oz can chicken broth
1 tablespoon Italian parsley
1 tablespoon chervil
⅔ cup Parmesan cheese
1 cup milk

Cook the onion in the olive oil until the onion is translucent. Add the garlic and cook for one minute. Add the potatoes, corn and chicken broth together until the potato is tender, 15-20 minutes. Add the milk, cheese, and herbs and heat until hot. Serves 4.

Mexican Chicken Soup

1 tablespoon olive oil
1 onion, chopped
2 cloves garlic, chopped
3 cups chicken broth
2 cups pureed tomatoes
1 cup corn
1 cup sliced carrots
1 green pepper, chopped
1 jalapeño (or more to taste), chopped
1 cup cooked chicken, shredded
1 tablespoon fresh oregano, chopped
1 tablespoon fresh cilantro, chopped
1 cup cheddar cheese

In a soup pot, cook the onion in the oil until tender. Add the rest of the ingredients, except the cheese. Cook until the vegetables are tender. Spoon into bowls and top with cheese before serving. Serves 4.

Grilled Corn

Pull back the husks to remove the silk from the ears of corn. Do not remove the husks. Replace the husks over the corn.

Submerge the ears in cold water and soak for at least one hour.

Place the ears of corn directly on the grill, making sure the husks cover the kernels completely. Turn the ears. They should cook in 5 to 10 minutes, depending on the heat of the coals.

Caution: The corn is extremely hot; be careful when pulling back the husks. The outside husks may get burnt, but the corn inside should be fine.

Cucumbers

Most people don't have the garden space for a lot of sprawling vines. I recommend the bush cucumbers, those with shorter vines. I've had luck with Bush Champion. The longer vined varieties can be grown on trellises to save space. Picklers are bumpy (Homemade Pickles) and slicers are smooth (Marketmore). Burpless varieties have a more mild flavor (Sweet Success is also seedless).

Planting: Plant 3-5 seeds in a square foot, one inch deep when the ground is warm, leaving about 4 feet (or more) between rows.

Thinning: Cucumbers spread, so thin them to at least 1 foot between plants. I usually plant about 5 seeds, which I thin to just one healthy plant (that will probably produce enough cucumbers).

Harvesting: Don't let the cucumbers get too big. Harvest them frequently (perhaps every other day at the height of the growing season). Pull them gently from the plant.

Preparing: Rinse, slice and eat. Peel the bigger cucumbers, which tend to have thicker skins. Add to salads or sandwiches.

Refrigerating: Cucumbers keep in the fridge for a couple weeks.

Helpful Hint: Keep those cucumbers picked! Then the plants will keep producing, so you'll have plenty to share with friends.

A Healthy Dose: One half cup of cucumber slices with the peel has 6 calories and .4 gram of fiber as well as 111 IU of vitamin A.

Historical Notes: Modern cucumbers originate from an ancient gourd, which grew in Africa and Asia.

Recipe

Cucumber Salad

> **2 cups, peeled, seeded, and chopped cucumbers**
> **1 tablespoon cider vinegar**
> **2 tablespoons lemon juice**
> **1 tablespoon lime juice**
> **2 teaspoons sugar**
> **¼ teaspoon salt**
> **3 tablespoons chopped parsley**
> **Optional: Add one more tablespoon of fresh chopped basil, cilantro, or dill.**

Combine the cucumbers with the vinegar, lemon juice, sugar, and salt. Stir in the parsley. Add the optional herbs. Chill. Serves 4.

Creamy Cucumbers

1 sliced cucumber
½ cup sour cream
1 tablespoon fresh dill

Combine all ingredients. Chill. Serves 2.

Vinegar Cucumbers

1 sliced cucumber
¼ cup vinegar
2 tablespoons sugar

Combine all ingredients. Chill. Serves 2.
Note: Experiment with different vinegars, such as raspberry or balsamic.

Cucumber and Sweet Pepper Salad

8 large cucumbers, peeled & sliced
1 large onion, sliced
1 cup diced celery
1 green pepper, diced
1 red pepper, diced
1 tablespoon salt
2 cups sugar
1 cup white vinegar
1 teaspoon celery seed
1 teaspoon mustard seed

Mix cucumbers, celery, onion, and peppers with the salt. Let it sit for 30 minutes. Drain. Stir together the sugar, vinegar, celery seed, and mustard seed until the sugar is dissolved and pour over cucumber mixture. Chill. This will keep three months in the fridge.

See Also
Radish: Radish and Cucumber Sandwich

Eggplant

Eggplants range in color a deep glossy purple to lighter shades and even pure white. Dusky is an early maturing purple eggplant. Green Goddess has a green, zucchini shaped fruit. Cloud Nine is white.

Planting: Since eggplants are warm weather vegetables, use transplants, planting 18 inches apart.

Harvesting: Look for smooth, shiny fruit. Pick them when they are the size described on the packet or insert. For example, Dusky will be 8-9 inches long, but Short Tom will only be 3-5 inches long. Overripe ones get soft. Pick carefully, since the cap of the eggplant is a bit thorny.

Preparing: If that eggplant looks old and might be bitter, cut the eggplant as the recipe requests and place it in a strainer in the sink. Salt the eggplant thoroughly and let it drain those bitter juices away. Rinse well to remove the extra salt.

Storing: Eggplants can be stored on the refrigerator for about a week.

Helpful Hint: Since eggplants (and tomatoes and peppers) need warmth, heat up the soil by covering it with black plastic.

A Healthy Dose: One cup of cooked, cubed eggplant has 27 calories and 2.4 grams of fiber as well as 245 milligrams of potassium.

Historical Notes: Eggplants, which are really berries, originated in southeast Asia.

Recipes

Grilled Eggplant

> **1 eggplant, sliced ½ inch thick**
> **½ cup Italian dressing**

In a bowl, coat the eggplant with the dressing thoroughly. Place the slices directly on the hot grill until lightly browned, turning once. Serves 2.

Note: This also works with zucchini, or try using the broiler instead of the grill.

Stuffed Eggplant

> **3 medium eggplants**
> **¼ cup green onions, sliced**
> **1 clove of garlic, chopped**
> **1 tomato, chopped**
> **1 tablespoon fresh oregano**
> **1 tablespoon fresh basil**
> **½ cup bread crumbs**
> **½ cup mozzarella cheese**

Slice the eggplants in half lengthwise, scooping out the pulp, but leaving a shell. Mince the eggplant pulp. In a skillet, cook the green onion, garlic, tomato and eggplant for about 15 minutes. Add the bread crumbs and herbs. Stuff the bread crumb mixture into the eggplant shells. Sprinkle with cheese and bake in 350° F oven for 35-45 minutes. Serves 6.

Vegetable Lasagne

This recipe doesn't call for noodles, but you may certainly add them.

> **1 eggplant, sliced and micro-waved until tender**
> **1 zucchini, sliced**
> **1 sweet pepper, sliced into strips**
> **1 onion, sliced into strips**
> **1 recipe easy marinara sauce**
> **2 cloves crushed garlic**
> **8 ounces ricotta cheese**
> **2 tablespoons chopped parsley**
> **8 ounces shredded mozzarella**

In a greased 9x13 pan, add ½ cup sauce and spread around the bottom. Layer the eggplant on the bottom. Stir the garlic into the ricotta. Spoon the ricotta on top of the eggplant. Add a layer of zucchini slices. Top with the onions and peppers and cover in sauce. Sprinkle the mozzarella cheese and parsley on top and cover. Bake in a 350° F oven 45 minutes, until the cheese is melted the center is hot.

Garlic

Garlic is best planted in the fall. Of the two types, softneck and hardneck, softneck, which is used for braiding, is the better for storage. Elephant garlic has a milder flavor.

Planting: In October, before the ground freezes, plant small cloves (separated from the larger bulb) 3 inches deep and large cloves 5 inches deep, 6 inches apart, in rich, loose soil. (Plant 3 times the size of the bulb deep). Bulbs can be planted in the spring, but they will be quite small. In the spring add a layer of compost to feed the plants.

Thinning: Garlic doesn't need thinning, but the central stalk should be clipped before a flower forms so that the energy goes into the bulb instead of the flower. The clipped greens can be eaten.

Harvesting: The long leaves of the bulb will turn yellow and wilt. Stop watering the plants for a few days before harvesting (this prevents mold). With a pitchfork, gently and carefully loosen the soil and left the entire plant from the soil. Wipe the dirt from the plant.

Preparing: In an airy place, let the plants cure (dry). Trim the roots and clean off any dirty spots. If you are braiding the garlic, keep the stems; otherwise, trim them. To use, simply peel the papery layers off a clove.

Storing: Store uncovered in a cool, dry, shady place.

Helpful Hint: Cover the planted cloves with a thick layer of compost or mulch in the fall. This protects the bulbs from the cold and feeds them in the spring.

A Healthy Dose: One clove of garlic has 4 calories.

Recipes

Garlic Butter

> 1 crushed clove of garlic
> 1 tablespoon chopped, fresh parsley
> ¼ cup (½ stick) softened butter

Stir the garlic (try two cloves if you're feeling brave) and parsley the butter. Spread on bread, crackers, or hot pasta. Store in the refrigerator (if there's any left).

Dill Dip with Fresh Garlic

> 8 oz. sour cream
> 1 crushed clove of garlic
> 2 tablespoons chopped, fresh dill

Combine and refrigerate.

Garlic Mashed Potatoes

These potatoes are not for those scared of garlic or calories.

7-8 large potatoes
3 cloves garlic
½ cup sour cream
¼ cup Parmesan cheese
¼ cup milk (or more)
2 tablespoons butter

Peel and cut the potatoes into chunks. Cook in boiling water until tender (15-20 minutes) and drain. Put the potatoes in large bowl. Crush the garlic over the potatoes with a garlic press. Add the milk, sour cream, and Parmesan. Mash or whip the potatoes until creamy (add more milk if needed). Dot the butter over the warm potatoes and serve. Serves 4.

Roasted Garlic

Clip the papery top of a whole head of garlic. Place it on a piece of aluminum foil, drizzle it with olive oil, wrap it, and roast in a 350° F oven until soft. Watch carefully. The garlic will be soft and moist and you should be able to push it right out of the papery shell. Spread on bread or crackers for a quick treat.

See Also

Asparagus: Asparagus Pasta with Pecans
Beans: Green Bean Casserole, Italian Chicken Soup
Broccoli: Broccoli Soup
Cabbage: Minestrone
Cauliflower: Cauliflower and Carrot Soup

Corn: Sweet Corn Soup, Mexican Chicken Soup
Eggplant: Stuffed Eggplant
Lettuce and Greens: Italian Style Vinaigrette
Okra: kra Stew
Peas: Peapod Stir Fry
Peppers: Ancho Beef Soup, salsas
Tomatoes: Italian Tomato Toss, Easy
     Marinara Sauce
Culinary Herbs: Tarragon Stew, Ultimate
     Flu Fighting Chicken Noodle Soup

Horseradish

The best thing you can do with horseradish is to make a sauce, and what a sauce it is! The flavor adds kick to lots of different foods, and its sinus-clearing properties are unique.

Planting: Prepare the soil by digging deeply and adding lots of compost. Plant the roots in the spring and keep watered. To treat this root as a perennial, leave part of the plant in the ground each fall.

Harvesting: Dig up the roots in the fall, usually after frost has killed the above-ground leaves.

Preparing: Shred or grate the root and preserve in vinegar. Add salt if you like. For English Horseradish Sauce, grate 2 tablespoons of the root into 2 tablespoons of lemon juice. Stir in ½ cup heavy cream. Too thick? Add some olive oil. Be careful; this is a pungent vegetable.

Storing: If kept cool and dry (in a bag in the fridge, for example), these roots will last a long time.

Helpful Hint: Horseradish grows very well, so plant it in a spot where it won't overwhelm more delicate plants.

Jerusalem Artichoke

Jerusalem artichokes, also called sunchokes, are members of the sunflower family. They are grown primarily for their nutty-tasting tubers.

Planting: Plan for a tall plant in the landscape—up to 8 feet tall. Plant the tubers 4 inches deep, about 2 feet apart. Use lots of compost, and add fertilizer or compost throughout the growing season.

Harvesting: In the fall, carefully dig up the plants for their roots.

Preparing: The tubers can be eaten raw in salads or cooked. Be careful not to overcook, as the tubers can get tough.

Storing: Store these tubers like potatoes, in a cool, dry place.

Helpful Hint: Clip the flowers so the plants grow bigger tubers.

A Healthy Dose: One cup of sliced Jerusalem artichokes has 114 calories and 2.4 grams of fiber as well as 643 milligrams of potassium and 21 milligrams of calcium.

Historical Notes: This plant is native to America and not related to artichokes. Explorers brought the plant to Italy, where was called "girasole," which has been anglicized as "Jerusalem."

See Also
   Brussels Sprouts: Brussels Sprout Soup
   Carrots: Carrot Stew
   Celery: Blasted Veggie Soup
   Parsnips: Trish's Root Vegetable Chicken Soup
   Rutabaga: Roasted Root Vegetables, New
      England Boiled Dinner

Kohlrabi

Kohlrabi is an early vegetable with a mild cabbage-like taste. Grand Duke and early White Vienna will do well in Minnesota as will Kolibri, which has a purple exterior and white interior.

Planting: Kohlrabis do best in cooler weather, so use transplants, but you may also have success with seeds. Plant about 10 inches apart. Mulch the plants well since kohlrabies like cool and moist soil.

Harvesting: Cut the swollen bottom from the root when it's about 2 inches around. Smaller is okay, but much larger and the vegetable gets woody.

Preparing: Wash, slice and eat. If the skin is tough, peel it. Kohlrabies can also be simmered in water until tender.

Storing: Store in the refrigerator for about a week.

Helpful Hint: Kohlrabi, like broccoli, can be planted at the end of summer for harvest in the fall.

A Healthy Dose: One cup of Kohlrabi has 356 calories and 4.8 grams of fiber as well as 32 milligrams of calcium and 83 milligrams of vitamin C.

Recipes

Kohlrabies are a great addition to the snack platter. Serve them with this or any other dip.

Kohlrabi with Red Pepper Dip

> 1 container cream cheese, softened
> ½ cup finely chopped sweet red pepper
> 1 small garlic clove, finely minced
> 2 tablespoon chopped fresh chives
> 2 tablespoons milk

Mix the ingredients together and refrigerate until ready to serve. Serve with strips of peeled kohlrabi.

Lettuce and Greens

Lettuces and greens are the mainstay of my spring garden. They grow fast and taste better than anything you can buy at the store. Looseleaf lettuce is very easy to grow and comes in a variety of shapes and a palette of greens and reds. Some varieties include Black-Seeded Simpson, Red Sails, and Green Ice. Some oakleaf type lettuces give an interesting look to a salad; Red Salad Bowl is one. Buttercrunch, one of my favorites, is one of the butterhead lettuces, which take a bit longer to mature. Crisphead and Romaine lettuces take the longest to mature but they are worth it. Summertime is an iceberg crisphead. For a Romaine variety, try Little Gem, which is small but matures quickly; Trout's Back is green with red speckles.

But lettuce is only one way to eat a salad. For a mild addition to your salad, I recommend Mâche, or corn salad. Also try fresh spinach, picking the baby leaves. For a zestier salad, add arugula, which is very easy to grow (for less tanginess, make sure to harvest these leaves when they are around 4 inches). Two more tangy greens are mustard and cress. Radicchio, related to chicory, is a colorful plant often seen in Italian salad blends. Endive (frisee), when properly grown, should be tied together for a blanched head, but I can't wait that long so I harvest the young leaves for my salads.

Once the leaves get large (and not as tender), these greens are perfect for cooking: mustard, spinach, Swiss chard. Some greens are grown for cooking, such as collards, kale and pac choi (or bok choy), though they can be eaten fresh as well.

Many garden catalogs offer "mesclun" mixes, which are different kinds of greens mixed together for growing an instant salad.

Planting: Most greens do better in cooler weather. Plant early, as soon as the ground can be worked. To extend the harvest of lettuce and other quickly maturing greens, plant at two-week intervals. For a fall crop, plant again in August. Seeds should be lightly covered with soil, planted one inch apart in rows 18 inches apart. (See the helpful hint for an alternative.) Note: spinach sprouts look a little like grass; mark your row clearly so you don't pull them by mistake.

Thinning: For large plants, thin to 12 to 18 inches between plants. The thinnings are edible.

Harvesting: Pick the leaves young and small to avoid bitter-tasting salads. Once the plants bolt (flower and go to seed), the leaves become bitter. Warm weather encourages bolting. Harvest the entire plant in warm weather, or harvest just the outer leaves to extend the crop in cooler weather.

Preparing: Rinse well, checking for sand and slugs. Dry using a salad spinner, or even a clean cotton towel.

Refrigerating: I like to harvest only what I use, since lettuces don't store very well. But it will keep for a few days in a covered container in the fridge.

Helpful Hint: Instead of large plants in rows, try scatter a variety of seeds in smaller, square area without rows. Harvest the small, young leaves for a tender salad.

A Healthy Dose: One half cup of shredded looseleaf lettuce has 5 calories as well as 538 IU of vitamin A. One cup of spinach has 6.6 calories and .8 gram of fiber as well as 29 milligrams of calcium and 2014 IU of vitamin A.

Recipes

Beautiful Summer Salad

Is it the summer or the salad that's beautiful? It doesn't matter because I am delighted when the greens come from my garden instead of the grocery store.

> **2 cups mixed greens: romaine, leaf lettuces including red oakleaf, endive, mache, baby chard, spinach, or whatever greens are in your garden**
> **1 chive blossom**
> **vinaigrette**
> **edible flowers for garnish (such as pansies or nasturtiums)**

Clean and dry the greens, placing them on a plate. Separate the chive blossom and sprinkle on the top. Dash with vinaigrette. Garnish with flowers. Serves 2.

Basic Vinaigrette

> **Oil: ½ cup**
> **Sour: ⅓ cup**
> **Sugar: 1 tablespoon**
> **Seasonings**

A basic vinaigrette combines oil, vinegar and seasonings. Olive oil is my preference for the oil. The sour could be fruit juice or vinegar. Try orange, lemon, or lime juices. Try cider, balsamic, or flavored vinegars. Sugar is necessary to balance the vinegar's acidity. For seasonings, try basic salt and pepper or get adventurous: fresh garlic, parsley for color, dill for some sweetness, oregano, cilantro, hot or sweet peppers, dry or Dijon mustard, or even fruit puree (like raspberries). Experiment for new taste sensations.

Italian-style Vinaigrette

> **½ cup olive oil**
> **⅓ cup balsamic vinegar**
> **1 tablespoon sugar**
> **1 clove garlic, crushed**
> **1 tablespoon fresh basil, chopped**
> **1 tablespoon fresh oregano, chopped**
> **1 teaspoon Dijon mustard**
> **a pinch of hot pepper flakes**

Whisk (or shake) the ingredients together. Store leftovers in the fridge. Olive oil will firm in the fridge, so bring the vinaigrette to room temperature before using.

Grilled Chard and Cheese Sandwich

1 oz reduced fat marble jack cheese, sliced
2 slices whole grain bread
1 Swiss chard leaf (or several small leaves)
1 large tomato slice (or several small ones)
light margarine

Place the chard leaf on one slice of the bread. Feel free to rip the edges so the chard fits. Add a layer of cheese. Add a layer of tomato. Add the last slice. Lightly spread the margarine on the outside of the sandwich. Cook over medium heat flipping once carefully until both sides are lightly browned and the cheese is melted. Serve hot.

Note: Add olives, sautéed mushrooms, or other vegetables as you like. Also, you may substitute spinach for the chard.

Spinach Raspberry Salad

Salad: 4 cups spinach leaves, washed, dried,
and torn into bite-sized pieces
1-2 cups raspberries
½ cup Bermuda onions rings
Dressing: ¾ cup mayonnaise
⅓ cup sugar
2 tablespoons raspberry vinegar
1 tablespoon poppy seeds

Blend the dressing ingredients together. Pour over the salad. Serves 4.

Note: This also works with strawberries.

Orange Spinach Salad

4 cups spinach, washed, dried, and torn
into bite-sized pieces
1 can mandarin oranges
½ teaspoon ground ginger
¼ teaspoon pepper
1 tablespoon vinegar
1 tablespoon olive oil
¼ cup toasted slivered almonds

Drain the juice from the oranges, reserving two tablespoons. Mix together the juice, ginger, pepper, vinegar, and oil. Pour over and toss with the spinach and oranges. Sprinkle with the almonds. Serves 4.

Spinach and Crab Salad

4 cups spinach, washed, dried, and torn into bite-sized pieces
8 ounces imitation crab meat
2 ounces feta cheese, crumbled
1 cup chopped green onions
dash of black pepper
dash of red pepper flakes
2 tablespoons salad dressing (such as blue cheese)

Combine the cheese with the black pepper and red pepper flakes. Toss with the rest of the ingredients. Serves 4.

Try adding celery or water chestnuts for extra crunch.

Baked Spinach Cheese Omelet

3 eggs, lightly beaten
1 cup cottage cheese
1 cup shredded mozzarella cheese
½ tablespoon olive oil
4 cups spinach, chopped
1 cup carrots, finely chopped
¼ teaspoon black pepper
1 tablespoon dill
1 tablespoon chives
1 tablespoon parsley
1 tablespoon chervil
2 tablespoons Parmesan cheese

Mix together eggs, cottage and mozzarella cheeses. Lightly sauté the spinach and carrots in the olive oil (about 2 minutes). Cool. Mix together the eggs and cheese, spinach and carrots, and the herbs. Pour into a 9 inch pie pan that has been sprayed with nonstick cooking spray. Sprinkle with the Parmesan cheese. Bake in a 350° F oven for 25 –35 minutes. Serves 4.

Okra

While this is a plant that needs hot weather, okra can be grown in Minnesota. Cajun Delight is an early maturing variety that works here.

Planting: After digging in a generous amount of compost, plant transplants 18-24 inches apart when nighttime temperatures are around 60 degrees F.

Harvesting: Pick the pods when they are 2½ inches long, about 4 to 6 days after blossoming. Bigger pods are less tender.

Preparing: Cut off the stem before cooking. Okra is best fried or cooked in a stew, like gumbo.

Storing: Okra can be stored in the refrigerator. Okra can also be cut and frozen.

Helpful Hint: The plant will stop producing blossoms if the pods are left on the plant to mature.

A Healthy Dose: One cup of okra has 33 calories and 3.2 grams of fiber as well as 81 milligrams of calcium and 88 mcg of folate.

Historical Notes: Okra, a member of the mallow family, originated in Africa.

Recipes

Deep Fried Vegetables

> vegetable oil for frying
> ½ cup milk
> 1 egg
> ½ teaspoon hot chili powder
> ¾ cup flour
> vegetables, such as okra, cauliflower, onion,
>   zucchini, etc., cut in small or thin pieces

Heat one inch of the oil. Mix together the egg and the milk. Stir in the chili powder and flour. Dip the vegetables in the batter and carefully fry them, turning once. Try not to crowd the pan. Most vegetables take about 2 minutes per side. Drain on paper towels.

Okra Stew

This is my version of gumbo without making a roux.

> 1 pound Cajun style sausage, cooked, sliced,
>   and deeply browned
> 1 tablespoon olive oil
> 1 green pepper, chopped
> 1 onion, chopped
> 2 stalks celery, chopped
> 4 cloves garlic, finely minced
> 1 ½ cups okra, sliced
> 3-4 large tomatoes, chopped
> 1 cup chicken broth
> ⅛ teaspoon black pepper
> ¼ teaspoon cayenne pepper
> ¼ cup water or chicken broth
> 2 tablespoons corn starch
> 2 cups hot cooked rice

In the olive oil, cook the green pepper, onion, and celery until the onion is translucent, 8-10 minutes. Add the garlic for one minute. Add the sausage, tomatoes, okra, chicken broth, and spices. Simmer for 15-20 minutes, until the okra is tender.

Stir the corn starch into the water, then stir the mixture into the bubbly stew to thicken. Spoon the stew into a bowl and top with a scoop of rice.

Onions

Since Minnesota's growing season is so short, buy plants or "sets" to plant in the early spring. Most garden centers offer the basic yellow, white or red onions. For a more specific variety, try day-neutral Candy or Superstar for big, sweet onions. Red Burgermaster is a long day variety. (Long day varieties grow green until the longest day, when bulb development begins.)

Planting: Plant these early! Plant one set every 2-3 inches. Onions are heavy feeders, so add lots of compost or organic fertilizer.

Thinning: Feel free to pull an onion to use its green top early in the season.

Harvesting: The green onion leaves will wilt, and the large bulb will be visible. With a pitchfork, loosen the soil and pull the plants gently. Let them sit in a warm, dry place for a few days. Clean any dirty spots and remove the roots and tops.

Preparing: Peel and slice or chop. Green onions are a great addition to scrambled eggs or omelets.

Storing: Store uncovered in a cool dry place.

Helpful Hint: For green onions, plant several sets together in a small hole, harvesting when the plants are long and green.

A Healthy Dose: One cup of chopped onion has 60 calories and 2.8 grams of fiber as well as 32 milligrams of calcium.

Historical Notes: Ancient Egyptians grew onions.

Recipes

Green Onion Stir Fry

This is the first meal my husband cooked for me.

> **½ pound boneless, skinless chicken breasts, cut into strips**
> **1 tablespoon olive oil**
> **2 cups cooked rice**
> **1 tablespoon soy sauce**
> **½ cup thinly sliced green onions**
> **2 eggs, lightly beaten.**

Cook the chicken strips in the oil until lightly brown and cooked thoroughly. Add the rice, soy sauce, green onions. Push the rice to the edge of the pan, scramble two lightly beaten eggs in the center, and then stir thoroughly until the eggs are completely cooked. Serves 2.

Marlyne's Bar-B-Q Roast Beef

Marlyne served this to me the first time I met her at the farm. With stored onions, this is good winter dish.

> **1 4-6 lb. chuck roast**
> **1 package dry onion soup mix**
> **1 can cream of mushroom soup**
> **1 cup barbeque sauce**
> **1 onion, chopped**

Pour soups, sauce, and onion over roast in a crock pot. It takes about 12-14 hours if the roast is frozen. Turn heat on high for about an hour, and then turn on low.

Easy Homemade Pizza

1 1lb loaf frozen bread dough, thawed
1 cup Easy Marinara sauce or pizza sauce
½ onion, chopped
½ green pepper, chopped
1 8-oz bag shredded mozzarella or pizza cheese

Spread the thawed dough on a lightly greased pizza pan (or a cookie sheet or a 9x13 inch cake pan). Using a fork, poke the dough at intervals. Bake for 10 minutes at 350° F. Spread the sauce on the crust. Add the chopped vegetables and the cheese. Bake for 10-15 minutes at 400° F until the cheese is bubbly. Serves 6.

Note: Add other vegetables as desired. If you prefer more tender veggies, steam or microwave them before placing them on the pizza.

See Also

Onions work well with almost every veggie; here are some highlights.

Beans: Green Bean Casserole, Cold green
    Bean Salad, Italian Chicken Soup, Chili
Okra: Okra Stew
Peppers: Ancho Beef Soup, salsas
Sweet Potatoes: Sweet Potato Soup
Squash: Stir Fried Zucchini and Green Onions
Tomatoes: Italian Tomato Toss, Easy
    Marinara Sauce

Parsnips

Parsnips store well and can be used like carrots. Harris' Model and All-American are two earlier maturing varieties.

Planting: Parsnips do best in a soil that is lower in nitrogen. The roots grow deeply, so dig the soil so it is loose and free of rocks. Since they are slow to germinate, mark the row. Sit back and relax, since they take a while to grow.

Thinning: Parsnips should be thinned so they are 3 inches apart.

Harvesting: After a frost to sweeten the roots, dig carefully since the parsnips are long.

Preparing: Prepare like carrots: peel, slice into thin rounds, and steam. Add butter, and/or pepper, if you like. Parsnips are good in recipes for root vegetables.

Storing: Parsnips store well in the refrigerator. Brush extra dirt off the roots (don't wash) and store in a loosely closed plastic bag.

Helpful Hint: I cover a newly planted row of parsnips with the lightest touch of straw mulch to aid germination by keeping the seeds moist and the soil soft.

A Healthy Dose: One cup of slices has 100 calories, 6.4 grams of fiber as well as 48 milligrams of calcium and 499 milligrams of potassium.

Recipes

Roasted Parsnips and Carrots

> **1 cup sliced parsnips**
> **1 cup sliced carrots**
> **1 tablespoon olive oil**
> **1 tablespoon fresh thyme**

Roast in a 350° F oven until the vegetables are tender, about 25 minutes.

Tricia's Root Vegetable Chicken Soup

> **2 tablespoons olive oil**
> **3 cloves garlic, minced**
> **3 medium carrots, cut in rounds**
> **2 small-medium parsnips, cut in rounds**
> **1 medium rutabaga, diced**
> **2 small turnips, diced**
> **2 medium potatoes, diced**
> **5 cans chicken stock**
> **3 tablespoons lemon juice**
> **2 tablespoons fresh tarragon**
> **2 cups cooked chicken breasts, diced**
> **1½ cups egg noodles**
> **3 leeks, white and pale green parts only,**
> **cut in rounds**

Using a large stock pot, heat 2 tablespoons olive oil and minced garlic. Add carrots, parsnips, rutabaga, turnips, and potatoes. Sauté on medium heat for about 5 minutes. Add the chicken stock, lemon juice, tarragon, and cooked chicken. Simmer until root vegetables are tender (about 20 minutes).

Add egg noodles and leeks. Simmer 10 minutes or until egg noodles are tender. Add salt and pepper to taste, if desired.

See Also

> Brussels Sprouts: Brussels Sprout Soup
> Carrots: Carrot Stew
> Celery: Blasted Veggie Soup
> Rutabaga: Roasted Root Vegetables,
> New England Boiled Dinner

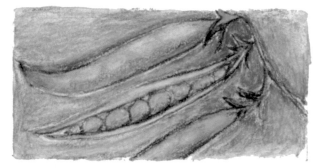

Peas and Peapods

Peas are a sweet treat. Shelling peas (without edible pods) need a lot of plants for a meal, but are much better garden-fresh than any canned concoction. Try Green Arrow and Wando. Snap peas are eaten, pod and peas together. Try Super Sugar Snap. Snow peas are harvested before the peas begin to form and are often used in stir-fries. Try Oregon Sugar Pod II.

Planting: Peas are a cool weather plant and should be planted just as soon as the soil can be worked. Plant peas just under an inch deep, 4 inches apart. Most peas need something to climb. I like to use bamboo stakes and twine to make a little trellis.

Thinning: Peas need air circulation. Also, mulch around the plants because it's tough to weed the vines as they grow. Pull the plants when they wither from the hot sun.

Harvesting: Harvest shelling peas and snap peas when their pods swell with the peas inside. Harvest snow peas when they are about 4-5 inches long, without the peas swelling. Younger snow pea pods are more tender than the older ones with thicker skins and swelled peas. Pull gently from the vine. Peas often will continue to produce with the right conditions (cooler weather).

Preparing: For peas, open the shell, remove the peas, and rinse. For pea pods, rinse (some snap peas may need a string near their stem removed). Steam about one minute, until bright green. Watch carefully while cooking; mushy peas and pea pods don't taste very good.

Refrigerating: Store in covered container for a few days.

Freezing : For peas, shell and rinse. For pea pods, remove blossoms or strings and rinse. Place in boiling water for 1-1½ minutes. Cool immediately in ice water. Drain completely and freeze.

Helpful Hint: A new recipe trend is stir-fried pea tendrils. Clip the top 6 inches of the sugar or snap pea plants when they are tender and disease-free.

A Healthy Dose: One cup of peas has 117 calories and 7 grams of fiber as well as 58 milligrams of vitamin C. One cup of pea pods has 26 calories and 1.6 grams of fiber as well as 37 milligrams of vitamin C.

Historical Notes: Before the sixteenth century, peas were eaten dried and cooked, like lentils, rather than fresh off the vine.

Recipes

Peapod Stir Fry

1 tablespoons of olive oil
2 cloves of garlic, sliced
3 cups of snow or snap pea pods

For one minute, stir fry the garlic in the oil. Add the pea pods. Stir fry until the pods are bright green and tender-crisp. Serves 3.

Sweet Green Pea Soup

1 tablespoon olive oil
1 sliced onion
1 chopped potato
1 14 ½ oz can chicken broth
4 cups peas, divided
1 tablespoon parsley, chopped
1 tablespoon mint leaves, chopped
1 cup half and half

Cook the onion in the olive oil until tender. Add the potato and broth. Cook until the potato is tender, about 15 minutes. Add 2 cups of the peas for about 3 minutes, until bright green. Blend the soup (with the center of the top of the blender removed) in small batches. Return the soup to the pot. Add the remaining peas, the milk, the mint, and the parsley and heat until hot, stirring frequently (do not boil). Serves 4.

Fresh Peas with Basil

Add as much basil as you like!

1 glove of garlic, finely chopped
1 tomato, diced
2 sprigs of basil, ripped into small pieces
2 cups of fresh peas

Combine the garlic, tomato, and basil. Bring a pot of water to boil. Place the peas into a strainer and dip the strainer into the water for one-two minutes, until the peas are bright green. Remove strainer with the peas and shake off the excess moisture. Stir the peas into the tomato mixture and serve.

See Also
Asparagus: Spring Pasta Salad
Mushrooms: Mac and Cheese with
Mushrooms and Peas

Peppers: Hot and Sweet

Every year, I look forward to my harvest of peppers, sweet and crispy...or hot and spicy. Buy early maturing varieties from your garden center. Growing from seed is necessary for some of the more exotic varieties and is worth it. Sweet peppers come in all colors: ivory (White Perfection or Ivory), red (North Star—good for northern Minnesota), orange (Orange Belle), yellow (Golden Bell), purple (Purple Beauty), and "brown" (Sweet Chocolate). Hot peppers range from mild (Ancho—a favorite) to hotter (Cayenne, Jalapeno) to hottest (Habanero).

Planting: Plant transplants 18 inches apart. Planting from seed directly into the garden is possible, but I suggest starting the seeds indoors instead.

Harvesting: Peppers can be picked any time after they are fully developed. Green peppers are good but have less flavor than when the peppers are in full color. Hot peppers are milder when they are green.

Preparing: Wash, rinse, and slice, removing the stems, seeds, and ribs. Sweet pepper are great fresh in salads. Caution: When chopping hot peppers, the oils may get on your hands (and whatever you touch) to cause a burning sensation. Also, the seeds are the hottest tasting part, so for a milder taste, remove them before cooking.

Storing: Peppers store well in the refrigerator. Chop sweet peppers and freeze for later use in recipes. For long term storage of hot peppers, string the fresh peppers on strong thread and hang them to dry.

Helpful Hint: Dig up and pot a pepper plant and place it in a sunny window. Keep the peppers picked and watch for (and remove) bugs. The plant should last through the winter (maybe even longer).

A Healthy Dose: One cup of chopped red, sweet peppers has 40 calories and 2.9 grams of fiber as well as 283 milligrams of vitamin C and 8493 IU of vitamin A.

Historical Notes: The Aztecs made sauces with tomatoes and peppers, which are native to the Americas.

Recipes

Notes for the salsa recipes:

• To save time, try using a food processor to chop the ingredients.

• Fresh, uncooked salsas are a delicious way to combine the fruits of your garden labor and may be stored in the fridge for a few days. If you'd like to freeze salsa, cook it first, and then freeze it in serving-sized containers. Cooking does make the garlic flavor milder.

• If you want a salsa that's less "juicy," use Roma (plum) tomatoes since they contain less water.

• Salt is not always necessary since salsas are naturally flavorful.

• Experiment with the ingredients in your garden to make your own salsa recipe; try different colors of tomatoes or peppers.

• Serve salsa with chips, on hamburgers, with grilled chicken or fish, or with eggs.

Sue's Salsa

> **4 tomatoes, chopped**
> **½ onion, chopped**
> **3 cloves of garlic, chopped**
> **3 sprigs of cilantro, chopped**
> **salt to taste**
> **jalapenos (seeded and chopped) to taste**
> **juice of ¼ lemon**

Combine the ingredients. Refrigerate.

Sweet Pepper Salsa

1 yellow pepper, seeded and chopped
1 orange pepper, seeded and chopped
1 red pepper, seeded and chopped
1 green pepper, seeded and chopped
1 jalapeno pepper, seeded and chopped
6 green onions, chopped
8 tomatoes, chopped
6 cloves of garlic, chopped
¼ cup fresh basil, finely chopped
juice of ½ lemon
salt to taste

Combine the ingredients. Refrigerate.
Note: This mild salsa is good on soft tacos.

Green Salsa

2 ripe, green tomatoes
½ onion, chopped
1 green pepper, seeded and chopped
1 green jalapeno, seeded and chopped
1 clove garlic, chopped
2 tablespoons fresh parsley, chopped
juice of ½ lime

Combine the ingredients. Refrigerate.

Salsa Chicken

1 pound boneless, skinless chicken breasts
1 recipe Sue's salsa (or other salsa)

Spray a 9x13 baking pan with non-stick vegetable oil spray. Arrange the chicken in the pan. Pour the salsa over the chicken. Bake in a 350° F oven about 30 minutes, until the chicken is done and the juices run clear. Serves 4.

Ancho Beef Soup

½ pound sirloin steak, thinly sliced
1 tablespoon olive oil
1 onion, thinly sliced
6 cloves garlic, thinly sliced
½ -1 ancho pepper, thinly sliced (depending
   on how hot you want the soup)
2 potatoes, thinly sliced
5 cups beef broth
pepper to taste
1 cup milk
1 cup smoked gouda cheese

Brown the meat and onions in the oil. Add all the next ingredients except for the milk and cheese. Simmer until tender. Add the milk, just heating until hot. Sprinkle some of the cheese over each bowl before eating.

Green Pepper Jelly Bites

whole wheat crackers, such as Triscuits
savory flavored cream cheese, such as onion
   and chive or the Red Pepper Spread
   in the Kohlrabi section
green pepper jelly

Top each cracker with cream cheese and a dollop of green pepper jelly. To make green pepper jelly, follow the pectin directions with the following ingredients: pectin, 1 cup ground green peppers, ½ cup ground jalapenos, 1½ cups vinegar, 6½ cups sugar, and green food coloring (optional).

Fried Peppers and Sausage

1 pound bulk Italian style turkey sausage
1 onion, cut in bite-sized pieces
2 sweet peppers (any color), cut
in bite-sized pieces

Brown and drain the sausage. Remove excess fat from the pan, if necessary. In the same pan, stir fry the onion and peppers until tender. Add back the sausage and cook until hot. Serve this hot with rice or pasta, or on buns with a slice of cheese, or rolled in a tortilla.

See Also

Asparagus: Asparagus Pasta with Pecans
Cabbage: Vegetable Slaw
Eggplant: Vegetable Lasagne
Kohlrabi: Red Pepper Dip
Okra: Okra Stew
Potatoes: Picnic Potato Salad, Skillet Potatoes
Tomatillos: Salsa Verde
Mushrooms: Mushroom and Sweet Pepper
Quesadillas

Potatoes

Potatoes come in many delicious variations. Try something with red (Red Norland and Red Pontiac), or brown (Butte) skins, and red (All Red), blue (All Blue), or gold flesh (Yukon Gold). Fingerlings are tasty potatoes the size of a finger (Rose Finn Apple and Russian Banana). We've had excellent luck storing Kennebec, using the potatoes for seed the next spring.

Planting: Potatoes should be planted early. Plant about 4 inches deep in loose soil. Water well.

Harvesting: The vines die (turn yellow and fall over) when the potatoes are ready to harvest. With a pitchfork, loosen the soil around the plants carefully and search. Spread the potatoes out to dry, removing any soft, broken, or bruised ones before storing together.

Preparing: Potatoes can be cut into pieces and fried in oil. Or baked in a 350° degree oven. Or cut (peeling optional) and boiled for ten minutes before mashing with milk and butter.

Storing: Store in a cool, dry place, away from onions (they'll encourage sprouting).

Helpful Hint: Potatoes can be harvested earlier for "baby" potatoes (best with the red varieties).

A Healthy Dose: One baked potato with the skin has 220 calories and 4.8 grams of fiber as well as 844 milligrams of potassium.

Historical Notes: Potatoes were originally cultivated in the Andes Mountains around 1000 B.C.

Recipes

Potato Soup

> **1 onion, chopped**
> **1 tablespoon olive oil**
> **4 potatoes, peeled and cut in bite-sized pieces**
> **2 carrots, chopped**
> **1½ cups water**
> **2 tablespoons chopped fresh dill**
> **1 tablespoon chopped fresh parsley**
> **2 cups milk**

Cook the onion in the olive oil until tender. Add the potatoes, carrots, and water. Cook until the potatoes are tender. Add the parsley, dill, and milk. Heat until hot. Serves 4.

Note: I like a lot of dill in this soup. Try other herbs such as basil, chives, sage, or rosemary.

Traditional Potato Salad

> **4 cups cooked potatoes, peeled and cut into bite-sized pieces**
> **1 stalk celery, chopped**
> **½ onion, chopped**
> **1 hard-boiled egg, chopped**
> **¾ cup mayonnaise**
> **1 teaspoon mustard**

Mix together the mayo and the mustard. Toss with the other ingredients.

Note: Add other veggies, such as peas, peppers (hot or sweet), cucumbers, or radishes. Serves 4.

Lefse

The recipe for this Scandinavian delicacy comes from my husband's Norwegian family, who tend to eat their lefse a bit differently than those on my side of the family with Swedish heritage.

> **4 cups riced or mashed potatoes**
> **¼ cup oil**
> **¼ cup cream**
> **2 tablespoons sugar**
> **1 teaspoon salt**
> **2 cups flour**

Mix all together, cool. Make into patties (about 3-4 inches across). Roll on floured surface--a cloth-covered pastry board is very good. Use no more flour than you have to. Carefully lift the lefse with a lefse stick and place on heated lefse grill. Bake on each side until lightly browned. Lay it flat on a towel and cover with another towel to keep soft. Cool before storing or freezing.

Hot German Potato Salad

My grandmother made this for family gatherings at the lake cabin. We ate our meals gathered around a huge picnic table spread with fried chicken, fruit salad and this potato salad. Even though she made huge batches, it was the first dish that disappeared.

**6 cups cooked red potatoes, peeled
  and thinly sliced (about 3 pounds)
1 cup chopped onion
6 slices bacon
2 tablespoons flour
2 tablespoons sugar
1 teaspoon salt
⅛ teaspoon pepper
¾ cup water
⅓ cup vinegar
1 tablespoon chopped parsley**

In a large skillet, fry the bacon until crisp. Drain the bacon, reserving 1-2 tablespoon drippings. Crumble the bacon.

Fry the onion in the drippings until tender. Stir in the flour, sugar, salt, and pepper. Cook over low heat, stirring until bubbly. Stir in the water and vinegar. Heat, stirring constantly, until the mixture comes to a boil. Boil and stir one minute.

Carefully stir in the potatoes and the bacon. Spoon the mixture into a casserole dish. Garnish with parsley. Bake covered in 325° F oven until heated through, 35-45 minutes. Serves 6.

Oven Roasted Potatoes

**4 potatoes
1 tablespoon olive oil (optional)
½ teaspoon pepper
1 teaspoon garlic powder
¼ cup shredded Parmesan cheese
seasoned salt, optional**

Scrub the potatoes well. Cut the potatoes in half and then slice them. Toss them with the optional olive oil. Stir in the pepper, garlic powder, cheese, and optional salt. Pour into a 9 x 13 baking pan that has been sprayed generously with non-stick cooking spray. Bake in 400° F oven for 20 minutes until the potatoes are tender and lightly browned. Serves 4.

Twice Baked Potatoes

This is nice with left-over baked potatoes.

**4 large potatoes, baked and cooled
1 tablespoon butter
milk
½ cup chopped broccoli
1 cup reduced fat cheddar cheese**

Slice off a layer of each potato. Leaving a shell, scoop out the potatoes. Mash with the butter and enough milk to make the potatoes creamy. Add the broccoli. Scoop into the shell and sprinkle with the cheese. Bake at 375° F for 25-30 minutes, until hot. Serves 4.

Note: For variations, try adding bacon or other kinds of cheese.

Herbed New Potatoes

1 pound new red potatoes
2 tablespoons butter
1 tablespoon chopped fresh dill
1 tablespoon chopped fresh parsley

Scrub the potatoes well. Boil them for 20-25 minutes. Drain. Toss with the butter and herbs. Serves 4.

Note: Try other herbs such as basil, chives, sage, or rosemary.

Picnic Potato Salad

4 cups cooked potatoes, peeled and cut
**   in bite-sized pieces**
1 cup green onions, chopped
1 small red pepper, chopped
2 tablespoons lemon juice
2 tablespoons olive oil
1 tablespoon fresh dill

Combine the lemon juice, olive oil and dill. Toss with the potatoes, green onions and red pepper. Serves 4.

Note: Experiment with different herbs from your garden in this dish.

Skillet Potatoes

2 tablespoons olive oil
4 potatoes
1 onion, chopped
1 green pepper, chopped

Scrub the potatoes. Slice the potatoes in half lengthwise, and then in thin slices. In a large skillet, heat the olive oil and then add the onion, peppers, and potatoes.

Stir frequently until the potatoes are tender and lightly browned. Serves 4.

Note: Substitute other root vegetables for some of the potatoes, such as carrots, turnips or rutabagas. Make sure the sizes of the slices are similar for even cooking.

See Also

Corn: Sweet Corn Soup
Garlic: Garlic Mashed Potatoes
Peas: Sweet Green Pea Soup
Peppers: Ancho Beef Soup
Shallots: Cheesy Potatoes
Turnips: Fried Turnips
Culinary Herbs: Tarragon Stew

Pumpkins

Choose an early variety. Some are bred for eating (Small Sugar) and some for carving (Orange Smoothie) and some for both (Early Sugar or Pie). And some are bred for size (Dill's Atlantic Giant). For a small garden, look for short-vined and bush varieties (We-Be-Little and Jack-Be-Little), though the shorter vines are still pretty long (often 10 feet).

Planting: Dig a lot of compost into the spot for pumpkins since they are heavy feeders. Big pumpkins need frequent watering and frequent fertilization (organic fertilizer or an application of compost). Plant the seeds one or two inches deep. Transplanting is possible but difficult. Long-vined varieties can be grown on a very sturdy trellis.

Harvesting: After the pumpkins have turned orange, cut the fruit from the vine, leaving 3-4 inches of stem.

Storing: Store in a cool place away from moisture and freezing. For using in recipes, cut the pumpkin in pieces (seeds and skin removed), simmer 15 minutes, mash, measure the amount for favorite recipes, and store in an airtight container in the freezer.

Helpful Hint: To make pumpkin puree for use in recipes, cook chunks of pie pumpkin (seeds removed) skin side up on a greased cookie sheet in a 350 F oven until tender (about an hour). Cool. Remove the skin and puree the pumpkin in a blender. Substitute 1¾ cups puree for one 15 oz. can.

A Healthy Dose: One cup of cooked, mashed pumpkin has 49 calories and 2.7 grams of fiber as well as 2650 IU of vitamin A.

Historical Notes: A Native American cooking method for pumpkins was to place a whole pumpkin in the ashes of a fire, later scooping out the cooked pumpkin and adding maple syrup.

Recipes

Roasted Pumpkin Seeds

2 cups pumpkin seeds
1 tablespoon butter, melted
dash of salt, if desired

Clean and dry the pumpkin seeds. Toss the butter and seeds together. Place on a cookie sheet and bake in a 300° F oven for 45 minutes, stirring frequently, until golden brown.

Great Pumpkin Muffins

1½ cups pumpkin puree
½ cup butter or margarine, softened
1½ cups sugar
2 eggs
3 cups all purpose flour
½ teaspoon salt
1 tablespoon baking powder
2 teaspoons pumpkin pie spice
1 cup raisins

Beat the butter, sugar and pumpkin puree in a large bowl. Combine the dry ingredients. Add them to the butter mixture. Stir in the raisins. Do not over-mix. Pour into a muffin pan lined with 12 paper muffin cups. Bake in a 400° F oven for 21-23 minutes. Makes 12 large muffins.

Note: Substitute 1½ teaspoons cinnamon, ¼ teaspoon nutmeg and ⅛ teaspoon ground cloves for the pumpkin pie spice if you don't have it.

Pumpkin Soup

½ tablespoon butter
1 tablespoon fresh ginger, grated
1 ¾ cup pumpkin puree
1 cup milk or cream
pepper to taste

In a soup pan, warm the ginger in the butter. Add the puree and heat until hot. Stir in the milk and heat until hot. Serves 4.

Note: You may substitute cooked and pureed winter squash for the pumpkin.

Nutty Pumpkin Pie

½ recipe pie crust (see page 121 for recipe)
Bottom layer

1 egg
1½ cup pumpkin puree
½ cup sugar
1 teaspoon cinnamon
½ teaspoon nutmeg
⅛ teaspoon cloves

Top layer

1 egg
¼ cup corn syrup
¼ cup maple syrup
½ cup sugar
3 tablespoons melted butter
1 teaspoon vanilla
1 cup pecan halves

For the crust: Roll out and place the dough in a pie pan. For the bottom: Stir together 1 slightly beaten egg, pumpkin, sugar, and spices. Spread over the bottom of pie shell. For the top layer, mix the other egg, syrups, sugar, butter, and vanilla. Pour it over the pumpkin mixture. Sprinkle the pecans over the top. Bake in a 350° F degree oven 45-50 minutes or until filling is set.

Radishes

Radishes are a winter-weary gardener's delight. They grow fast and reliably, and though they are not terribly versatile, they are a taste of spring. French Breakfast is an oblong radish with a white tip. Easter Egg II radishes are one inch around in red, white and purple. Cherry Belle grows well in northern Minnesota. Daikon radishes, such as Summer Cross, can be grown in the fall.

Planting: Grow radishes in cool weather (they bolt quickly in hot weather). Plant seeds ½ inch deep, ½ inch apart. Water well.

Thinning: Thin to 1–1½ inches apart. Thinning is important to get large, fully shaped radishes.

Harvesting: Harvest quickly (most mature in 22-30 days) for the best radishes. Simply pull the plant from the ground.

Preparing: Remove the green top and the bottom, rinse and eat.

Helpful Hint: Once the radishes bolt (go to seed) they form a pod, which can be eaten.

A Healthy Dose: One small radish has .4 calories.

Recipes

Del's Radish and Cucumber Sandwich

> 1 radish, sliced
> ½ cucumber, sliced
> 4 slices of bread
> butter or margarine

Add slices of cucumber and radish to buttered bread.

Radishes and Black Beans on Rice

> 1 tablespoon olive oil
> red wine vinegar to taste
> 2 cups cooked black beans
> salt and pepper to taste
> 1 cup sliced radishes
> 2 finely sliced green onions
> 2 tablespoons chopped cilantro
> 2 cups hot cooked rice

In a small sauce pan, stir the oil and vinegar into the beans and stir gently until the beans are heated through. Add salt and pepper, if desired. Stir in the radishes and cilantro to the pan and cook for 1-2 minutes until the mixture is warmed through. Spoon the beans over the rice and sprinkle the green onions over the top.

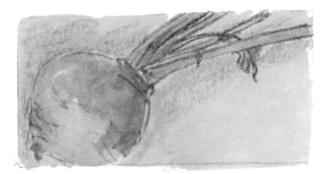

Rutabagas

American Purple Top and Laurentian are two early maturing varieties.

Planting: Plant seeds directly into the ground as soon as the soil is ready in spring, after digging in some compost. Keep the soil moist until the plants have germinated (which may take 20 days).

Thinning: Thin to 8 inches between plants.

Harvesting: In the fall, dig these large roots out of the ground.

Preparing: Peel, chop, and simmer until tender.

Storing: Store in a cool, dry place for use throughout the winter.

Helpful Hint: Substitute rutabaga for a portion of potatoes in mashed potatoes for a zippier flavor.

A Healthy Dose: One cup of cubed rutabagas contain 50 calories and 3.5 grams of fiber as well as 66 milligrams of calcium and 35 milligrams of vitamin C.

Historical Notes: Rutabagas are a cross between cabbages and turnips created by Casper Baudin in 17th century Switzerland.

Recipes

Roasted Root Vegetables

Fill a single layer of a 9x13 inch pan with any of the following, cut into bite-sized pieces:

> **rutabagas**
> **potatoes**
> **celeriac**
> **parsnip**
> **carrots**
> **turnips**
> **sweet potatoes**

Toss with 2 tablespoons olive oil and salt and pepper to taste. Roast in a 350° F about 30 minutes, until the vegetables are easily pierced with a fork and lightly browned.

New England Boiled Dinner

Try just about any autumn or root vegetable, cut into large chunks for the traditional boiled dinner look. Go with more or less ham, more or fewer vegetables, depending on your personal taste.

> **1 rutabaga, cut into large chunks**
> **1 onion, quartered**
> **2 carrots, cut into large chunks**
> **2 potatoes, cut into large chunks**
> **2 parsnips, cut into large chunks**
> **2 cups large ham chunks**

Put all the ingredients in a large pot, bring to a boil, and simmer for about 30 minutes, until the vegetables are tender. Add black pepper to taste.

See Also
> Brussels Sprouts: Brussels Sprout Soup
> Carrots: Carrot Stew
> Celery: Blasted Veggie Soup
> Parsnips: Trish's Root Vegetable Chicken Soup

Shallots

Shallots taste like a mild onion but are shaped like large garlic cloves.

Planting: Separate the cloves, and plant them 6 inches apart, keeping the tip even with the soil line. Mulch well. Keep shallots evenly watered throughout the season.

Harvesting: When the tops die back, the shallots are ready to dig up.

Preparing: Peel and chop, cooking with the other ingredients in the recipe. Try substituting the mild shallot for onion and/or garlic in a recipe. Shallots add a nice flavor to scramble eggs.

Storing: Store shallots like onions. They may last two to three months.

Helpful Hint: Clip the green tops for flavoring recipes (similar to chives).

A Healthy Dose: One tablespoon of minced shallots has 7 calories as well as 119 IU of vitamin A.

Recipes

Ham and Shallot Pasta Toss

> 8 ounces pasta, such as penne
> 2 tablespoon olive oil
> 1 medium shallot, chopped
> 1 cup ham, chopped
> 1 cup shredded guyere cheese

While the pasta cooks, heat the shallot in the olive oil in a small pan. Add the ham and heat through. After draining the pasta, toss together the warm shallots and ham along with the cheese. Serve warm.

Cheesy Potatoes

If you don't have leftover baked potatoes, microwave the potatoes for about ten minutes, until they are easily pierced with a fork.

> 6-7 small potatoes, already baked, with skins on
> 2 cups sharp cheddar cheese
> 1 tablespoon olive oil
> 1 shallot, finely chopped
> ½ cup plain yogurt
> ½ cup milk
> black pepper to taste

Sliced the potatoes and place in a well-greased 2 quart baking pan. In a sauté pan, cook the shallot in the olive oil. Add the yogurt and milk, stirring until smooth. Pour the warm liquid evenly over the potatoes. Sprinkle the cheese over the top. Bake in a 375° F oven for 25-30 minutes until brown and bubbly.

Squash

Types of summer squash include Italian, yellow, and patty pan. The one ultimate Minnesota summer squash is zucchini—and most of us seem to have too much of it (thus the wide array of recipes). Still there are some interesting variations of zucchini. Yellow varieties are nice because it's easy to catch those fast-growing zukes; try Gold Rush. Choose a bush variety like Spacemiser if you are short on space.

Winter squash and gourds (luffa, for example) require a long, hot growing season so choose early maturing varieties. Acorn (Table Ace) and Butternut (Early Butternut) are good choices. Baby Blue Hubbard is blue outside and gold inside. Sweet Meat looks like a green pumpkin and can be used like one.

Planting: Plant the seeds one or two inches deep. Transplanting is possible (and perhaps necessary for later maturing varieties like ornamental gourds), but squashes don't like their roots disturbed. Squashes are vining veggies and can be grown on a very sturdy trellis, which is recommended for ornamental gourds to keep their shape.

Harvesting: Harvest summer squash when the fruits are small to medium sized. Larger fruits can be shredded for recipes. Blossoms can be deep-fried or added to salads. Let winter squash stay on the vine until they are mature. Protect the fruits from frost. Allow the gourds to cure in a cool, dry place.

Storing: Store in a cool place away from moisture and freezing (the fridge is good if you have room). For using in recipes, cut the winter squash in pieces (seeds and skin removed), simmer 15 minutes, mash and store in an airtight container in the freezer.

Helpful Hint: Use the large zucchini (the one that hid under the leaves for a week) for zucchini breads and cakes.

A Healthy Dose: One cup of sliced summer squash with the skin has 15 calories and 1.3 grams of fiber. One cup of cubed winter squash has 56 calories and 2.1 grams of fiber.

Historical Notes: The word "squash" has its roots in the Algonquian word "askutasquash," generally meaning members of the cucurbit family.

Recipes

Baked Winter Squash
with Butter and Brown Sugar

1 winter squash
2 tablespoons butter
2 tablespoons brown sugar

Cut the squash in half and remove the seeds. Bake in a 350°F oven, cut side down, for 30 minutes. Turn cut side up, cover, and bake 15-25 minutes longer, depending on the size of the squash. Remove the cover. Carefully spread the butter over the squash and sprinkle with the brown sugar. Broil for 1–2 minutes until the sugar is bubbly. Serves 2.

Note: Pumpkin can be substituted for the winter squash.

Zucchini Pancakes

2 cups zucchini, coarsely grated
2 eggs, beaten
2- 4 tablespoons minced onion
½ cup flour
½ teaspoon baking powder
½ teaspoon salt
¼ teaspoon oregano

Put zucchini in a strainer to drain excess moisture (about 1 hour). Combine zucchini, onion, flour, baking powder, salt and oregano. Stir in the egg. Fry in a skillet over medium heat, turning once (just like a pancake). Serves 2.

Stir Fried Zucchini and Green Onions

1 zucchini, sliced into rounds
3 green onions, sliced into rounds
1 tablespoon olive oil

Sauté the zucchini and onions in the oil until lightly browned. Serve immediately. Serves 2.

Rosie's Zucchini Bread

This is the one I grew up with, and it was so good I didn't understand what all the fuss was about too much zucchini.

3 eggs, well beaten
2 cups sugar
1 cup oil
3 teaspoons vanilla
3 cups grated zucchini
1 cup raisins
3 cups flour
1 teaspoon baking powder
1 teaspoon baking soda
¼ teaspoon salt
2 teaspoons cinnamon

Grease with nonstick cooking spray two 9½ x 5½ x 2¾ inch pans. Sift together flour, baking powder, soda, salt, and cinnamon. Set aside. Beat together eggs, sugar, vanilla, and oil. Stir in zucchini. Blend in dry ingredients. Stir in raisins. Bake in 350°F oven for one hour.

Chocolate Lover's Zucchini Cake

2 eggs
½ cup softened margarine
½ cup oil
1¾ cups sugar
½ cup buttermilk
½ cup cocoa
1 teaspoon cinnamon
½ teaspoon baking powder
1 teaspoon baking soda
1 teaspoon salt
2½ cups flour
2½ cups zucchini, shredded
1½ cups milk chocolate chips

Grease with nonstick spray a 9x13 inch pan. Sift together the cocoa, cinnamon, baking powder, soda, salt, and flour. Set aside. Cream together the oil, sugar, and butter. Blend in the eggs and milk. Add the dry ingredients. Stir in the zucchini. Pour into the pan. Sprinkle the cake with the chips. Bake at 325°F for about 50 minutes. Serves 12 (or one chocoholic).

See Also
  Cabbage: Minestrone
  Eggplant: Vegetable Lasagne

Tomatillos

The Salsa Verde at Mexican restaurants contains tomatillos. Try Toma Verde, Tomatillo, or Mexican Strain.

Planting: Like tomatoes, it's best to use transplants. Space the plants 2 feet apart, mulching well.

Harvesting: The husk will be papery, just opening to reveal a yellowish fruit.

Preparing: Remove the husk before eating. Green tomatillos are sometimes hard and should be simmered before eaten.

Storing: Tomatillos will keep longer if left in the husk.

Helpful Hint: Use a tomato cage to keep the plants and fruits off the ground.

A Healthy Dose: One half cup of diced tomatillos has 18 calories and 1 gram of fiber as well as 20 milligrams of calcium and 14 milligrams of vitamin C.

Recipes

Salsa Verde

> **4 tomatillos, husks removed and diced**
> **2 jalapenos, diced**
> **1 large garlic clove, chopped**
> **½ onion, diced**
> **½ cup chicken broth**
> **¼ cup cilantro or parsley, chopped**

Simmer the tomatillos, the peppers, garlic and onion in the chicken broth until tender, about ten minutes. Remove from the heat. Add the cilantro. Blend until smooth.

Tomatoes

Every tomato lover has a favorite variety, but here's some general advice. For beginners, choose the most resistant varieties. The labels will have different letters, for example F1, F2, and V (for fusarium wilt, race 1 and 2, an verticulum wilt, race 1). Early Girl has a good combination of resistances. Basically, the more letters on the label, the more resistant the plant.

Heirloom varieties may not have the same resistances as the hybrids, but don't let that stop you from trying them. Brandywine is a tasty and popular heirloom. Determinate varieties are the "bush" type, and their harvest tends to happen all at one. Celebrity is a disease-resistant determinate variety. Indeterminate varieties will vine until frost kills them and their harvest is over a period of time. Try Sweet 100 for an indeterminate cherry tomato.

Paste or plum tomatoes are good for sauce and drying (La Rossa, Viva Italia, and Roma). And the colors! Green Zebra is a yellowish-green tomato with green stripes. White Wonder is a white tomato. Sun Gold has golden cherry tomatoes. Yellow Pear has tomatoes like, well, yellow pears. Cherokee Purple is a pinkish purple tomato. From tiny to tremendous, tomatoes are a Minnesota gardener's pride.

Planting: Use transplants. Tomatoes grown from seed in the garden often don't have enough time to produce a decent crop. Use a tomato cage or other staking system so the plants and fruit stay off the ground. Mulch the plants well to prevent water splashing soil-borne diseases on the leaves. Some swear that red plastic mulch increases yields, but I think those hot, humid summers are just what tomatoes need. Space the plants 2 feet apart.

If your tomatoes are having disease problems, try mulching even more thickly the next year. For best results, it's important to rotate tomato crops so they are not grown in the same space every year. This includes other nightshade family plants, like potatoes. Try a four year rotation in your garden.

Harvesting: Pull the ripened fruit off the vine gently. If frost is predicted, pull the remaining un-ripened tomatoes off the vine and place in a brown paper bag on the counter. Note: At the end of the season clean the remaining plants and fruits from your garden to help prevent disease the next year.

Preparing: Remove the core, slice and eat. My neighbor, Duane, takes the salt shaker out to the garden and eats until his heart…or his stomach…is content.

Storing: Do not refrigerate your tomatoes! Store them on the counter until they have been cut (and then if you have leftover slices, they can go in the fridge). For freezing (to use in recipes), remove the skins. (To remove the skins easily, boil whole, clean tomatoes for about half a minute until the skin starts to crack. Place immediately in cold ice water. Then the skins will peel off easily.) Place cut (or whole or pureed) tomatoes in an airtight container and freeze.

Helpful Hint: For long, spindly transplants, carefully remove the bottom leaves, place the roots and vine in a trench, leaving the leafy top above the soil line. Roots will grow on the vine underground.

A Healthy Dose: One cup of chopped tomatoes has 37 calories and 1.9 grams of fiber as well as 46 milligrams of vitamin C and 1121 IU of vitamin A.

Historical Notes: Tomatoes were once thought to be poisonous by northern Europeans. Later this indigenous American fruit was called the love apple because it was thought to be an aphrodisiac.

Recipes

Earl's Tomato and Peanut Butter Toast

I thought my dad was joking when he told me about this sandwich, but he enjoys it.

> 2 slices fresh white bread
> 2 tablespoons peanut butter
> 2 slices ripe tomato

Toast the bread. While it's still warm, spread the peanut butter. Add the tomato slices to make a sandwich. Serves 1.

Du's Tomato Sandwich

Duane, my father-in-law, has perfected this sandwich. Who am I to disagree?

> **2 slices fresh white bread**
> **margarine**
> **mayonnaise**
> **2 slices of ripe tomato**
> **lettuce, optional**
> **fried bacon slices, optional**

Toast the bread. Spread the margarine on both slices of the toast. Add the mayo on both slices. Add the tomatoes (and the optional bacon and lettuce) to make a sandwich. Serves 1.

Italian Tomato Toss

1 pound pasta, cooked and drained
1 onion, chopped
1 tablespoon olive oil
3 cloves garlic, sliced
4 tomatoes, chopped
¼ cup fresh basil leaves
1 cup mozzarella

In a large skillet, cook the onion in the olive oil until tender. Add the garlic and cook for one minute. Add the tomatoes and heat just until hot. Remove from the heat. Toss the pasta, basil, mozzarella, and tomato mixture together. Serve immediately. Serves 4.

Easy Marinara Sauce

1 onion, chopped
1 tablespoon olive oil
3 cloves garlic, sliced
6 tomatoes, chopped and peeled
1 container tomato paste
2 tablespoons fresh oregano
¼ cup fresh basil leaves

In a pot, cook the onion in the olive oil until tender. Add the garlic and cook for one minute. Add the tomatoes and simmer for at least 10 minutes. Add the tomato paste a little at a time to thicken the sauce. You may need less than a full container, depending on the juiciness of the tomatoes. If the sauce gets too thick, add a little bit of water. Add the herbs for the final minutes of cooking.

Note: Roma or plum tomatoes are traditionally used for sauces because they contain less water, but slicing tomatoes can be used as well. Some people like to remove the tomato seeds, but I find that too time-consuming. For a smoother sauce, run the cooked sauce through a blender and re-heat. Also, adding veggies to the sauce is delicious, such as diced eggplant, chopped broccoli, sliced carrots, sliced zucchini, or whatever else is ready in the garden.

Oven Roasted Tomatoes

Chop the cooked tomatoes for a quick sauce for pasta.

Tomatoes, preferably paste or plum,
sliced the long way
Olive oil
Fresh herbs (such as oregano, basil,
thyme, rosemary)

Line a baking sheet with sides with aluminum foil. Drizzle the tomatoes with olive oil and sprinkle with the fresh herbs. Bake in a 300° F oven until the tomatoes are hot and juicy and the skins look a little shriveled. Differences in tomatoes, such as size and level of ripeness will make a difference on how long these need to cook. Plan on half an hour, but be careful because they can get dried out if left in the oven too long.

Tomatoes and Fresh Mozzarella

Very ripe tomatoes, sliced
Fresh large basil leaves
Fresh mozzarella, sliced
Extra virgin olive oil
Red wine vinegar
Oregano
Pepper

Arrange the tomatoes, basil, and cheese on a platter. Drizzle and sprinkle the extra virgin olive oil, red wine vinegar, oregano, and pepper to taste.

See Also

Beans: Green Bean Casserole,
    Italian Chicken Soup
Beets: Vegetable Borscht
Broccoli: Summer Pasta Salad
Carrots: Carrot Stew
Corn: Mexican Chicken Soup
Lettuce and greens: Grilled Chard
    and Cheese Sandwich
Peas: Fresh Peas and Basil
Peppers: salsas
Culinary Herbs: Cilantro Sauce

Turnip

Purple Top White Globe is a typical turnip variety. Toyko Cross matures quickly, in about 30 days.

Planting: After digging in some compost, plant seeds directly into the ground as soon as the soil is ready in spring. Keep the soil moist until the plants have germinated (which may take 20 days).

Thinning: Thin to 6 to 8 inches between plants.

Harvesting: Dig the roots out of the ground. Smaller turnips are usually more tender; try for two inch diameters, certainly under three.

Preparing: Peel and simmer until tender.

Storing: Turnips keep well. Store in a cool, dry place for use throughout the winter.

Helpful Hint: Turnips' green tops can be eaten. Clip them any time during the season.

A Healthy Dose: One half cup of cubed turnips has 18 calories and 1 gram of fiber as well as 20 milligrams of calcium and 14 milligrams of vitamin C.

Historical Notes: Turnips may be one of the oldest vegetables, grown 5000 years ago.

Recipes

Fried Turnips

1 cup diced turnip
1 cup diced potatoes
½ onion, chopped
1 tablespoon olive oil
1 tablespoon butter

Melt the butter in a sauté pan. Stir in the rest of the ingredients and cook until the potatoes and turnips are tender.

See Also

Brussels Sprouts: Brussels Sprouts Soup
Carrots: Carrot Stew
Celery: Blasted Veggie Soup
Parsnips: Trish's Root Vegetable Chicken Soup
Rutabaga: Roasted Root Vegetables, New England
    Boiled Dinner

Culinary Herbs

Growing herbs is delightful, since they are ornamental as well as useful. Some herbs are better when they are fresh or frozen, such as basil, but the majority can be dried for future use.

When drying herbs, hang the whole plant upside down in a cool, dry, dark spot. Good air circulation is important to prevent mold. Also, avoid direct sunlight when drying and storing herbs.

Try drying herbs on a mesh sweater dryer if hanging space is limited, or dry them in a warm oven: After removing stems, place the herbs on a cookie sheet in a 200 degree F oven until just dry (watch closely!). Let the herbs cool completely before storing.

Basil

Basil is beautiful as well as tasty. It's one of the crops I most look forward to in the summer. The basic basil (Sweet, Italian) is familiar in pesto. Purple Ruffles is a deep, dark purple basil that makes a pretty border. Sweet Dani has a distinct lemon scent. Siam Queen Thai basil, perfect for stir-fries, has a slightly anise scent and in my opinion is the most beautiful basil plant.

Planting: This herb is best grown in well-drained soil and may be grown in a pot as well. Don't rush: be sure the soil is quite warm. To keep the seeds evenly moist, sprinkle a bit of compost or mulch very lightly on top of the seeds. For gardeners in a hurry, plants are the best bet.

Harvesting: Clip the top leaves of the plants. This keeps the plants bushy and compact.

Preparing. Chop or rip the leaves, adding them at the last minute since heat destroys the flavor.

Freezing: While it is possible to dry basil leaves, I chop handfuls of leaves with a bit of olive oil in my food processor. Then I freeze them in an ice cube tray. After they are frozen, I transfer them to a large plastic bag. Whenever I need a bit of basil, I pop a cube into the recipe.

Chervil

The flavor of chervil is as delicate as its lacy leaves.

Planting: This delicate-tasting herb is best grown in well-drained soil and may be grown in a pot as well. This plant may self-seed itself.

Harvesting: Harvest the plants' leaves before or during flowering.

Preparing: Chop the leaves. Add to soups or salads. Chervil makes delicious herbed butter.

A Healthy Dose: Traditionally used to help digestion or as a poultice for wounds.

Chives

I grow both regular chives (a mild, onion flavored herb) as well as garlic chives in my garden. This is a wonderful spring treat.

Planting: This herb is best grown in well-drained soil and may be grown in a pot as well. Use seeds or transplants. Note: Chives produce many, tiny seeds. If the plants spread too much, pop off the flower heads before they go to seed.

Harvesting: The long thin leaves of chives are used. They are best before and during the flowering of the plant.

Preparing: Clip a leaf with a scissors to make the O shape. The flowers may also be eaten and are pretty in a salad. I add fresh chives to already-cooked sweet corn.

Freezing: Chives are not very flavorful when dried, but they may be chopped and frozen in a freezer bag.

Cilantro/Coriander

The leaves of the plant are called cilantro; the seeds of the plant are coriander.

Planting: This herb is best grown in well-drained soil and may be grown in a pot as well. The plant may go to seed quickly, and if the plant is left to its own devices, it will probably self-sow.

Harvesting: For cilantro, clip the leaves before or during the flowering of the plant. For coriander, wait until the seeds have turned brown. For drying the seeds, clip the entire flower head into a paper bag and dry the seeds in a cool, dark place.

Preparing: Chop the leaves for recipes such as salsa. The seeds may be crushed or cracked, like pepper.

A Healthy Dose: Coriander has an ancient history (it's mentioned in the Bible) and supposedly helps digestion (1 teaspoon of crushed seeds for one cup of boiling water).

Dill

Dill weed is the leaves of the plant and can be used fresh in recipes. Dill seed is pretty self-explanatory. Some varieties are now available that are leafier for dill weed (Dukat) or smaller for container gardens (Fernleaf).

Planting: This herb is best grown in well-drained soil. My dill plants seed themselves so well that they turn up in every garden bed. I let them grow where they fall for attracting beneficial insects.

Harvesting: For the leaves, harvest early for mildest flavor. For seeds, harvest when the seeds have turned brown. Let some drop to the ground for early spring plants.

Preparing: I snip the leaves of the plant into recipes. Some people like to add the whole plant (roots removed) to their pickles.

 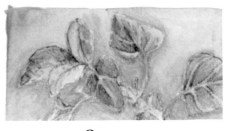 

Marjoram

Marjoram, also called sweet marjoram, is similar to oregano in its uses and grows as a perennial in very warm climates, so in Minnesota it's best grown in a pot indoors or as an annual outdoors.

Planting: This herb is best grown in well-drained soil and may be grown in a pot as well. Use seeds or transplants when the ground is warm.

Harvesting: Clip the leaves from the plant before or during flowering for the best flavor.

Preparing: Add fresh or dried leaves to recipes where you'd use oregano. Marjoram may be sweeter, though it's difficult to tell.

A Healthy Dose: Marjoram has the same uses as oregano as well as the possibility that it may inhibit growth of the herpes virus.

Oregano

Common oregano is tall and bold. My plant is growing extremely well—a little too well in its tiny spot. Greek oregano is low growing and more delicate tasting.

Planting: This herb is best grown in well-drained soil and may be grown in a pot as well. Use seeds or transplants when the ground is warm.

Harvesting: Clip the leaves from the plant before or during flowering for the best flavor.

Preparing: Add fresh or dried leaves to recipes.

A Healthy Dose: Although we think of oregano for pizza and pasta, oregano has been used for coughs and to help digestion. It's also considered an antiseptic for skin.

Parsley

Basic parsley (curled) is the garnish restaurants use and flat leaf or Italian parsley is more often used for its flavor. Planting: Parsley is a biennial, meaning it flowers the second year. Soak seeds before planting to aid germination, or buy the plants in the nursery.

Harvesting: Clip the leaves for use anytime.

Preparing: Parsley is best fresh, but I freeze some for use in recipes during the winter. Dried parsley loses its color and flavor.

A Healthy Dose: Parsley has a high concentration of chlorophyll, so chewing it helps freshen the breath. It may also be a diuretic.

Rosemary

Aromatic rosemary has a reputation for improving memory.

Planting: Unfortunately, rosemary does not survive Minnesota winters, but it can be brought indoors in a pot in the fall. Buy this herb in plant form, grow it in well-drained, sandy soil, and be careful not to over-water it.

Harvesting: Clip twigs from the plant and remove the leaves.

Preparing: The long thin leaves may be used whole or chopped. Rosemary may be dried in a cool, dark spot.

A Healthy Dose: This now culinary herb was once used for everything from warding off evil to curing paralysis.

Sage

Common sage has aromatic gray-green leaves. Pineapple sage has a pineapple smell.

Planting: This herb is best grown in well-drained soil and may be grown in a pot as well. Use seeds or transplants when the ground is warm. Be sure to mulch these plants well, since sage does not like extremely cold weather.

Harvesting: Clip leaves off the plant for use anytime. This plant can be dried for future use.

A Healthy Dose: Warm sage tea can be used as a gargle for a sore throat. Sage has been used to help digestion, as an antiperspirant, and a tooth powder.

Savory

Summer savory is an annual and winter savory is a perennial that may survive a mild winter in Minnesota.

Planting: Use seeds or transplants.

Harvesting: Clip the leaves as needed.

A Healthy Dose: Savory has been used as a cough remedy, but now it's mostly used in cooking.

Tarragon

Russian tarragon may be grown from seed, but French tarragon is the preferred variety and should be grown from a cutting or a plant from the nursery.

Planting: This herb is best grown in well-drained soil. Be warned: it loves to spread.

Harvesting: Clip the leaves for use anytime. This herb may be dried in a cool, dark spot, but the leaves are better fresh.

A Healthy Dose: Tarragon leaves were chewed in ancient times to alleviate oral pain.

Thyme

After a harsh winter, I often have to replant thyme. I love fresh thyme in soups.

Planting: Thyme is a low-growing, delicate looking plant. Some varieties do well in rock gardens. This herb is best grown in well-drained soil and may be grown in a pot as well. Use seeds or transplants when the ground is warm. Mulch well since thyme doesn't like the extreme cold.

Harvesting: Clip leaves for use anytime. This herb can be dried in a cool, dark spot for future use.

A Healthy Dose: Thyme has been used to help digestion and relieve coughs.

Herbal Recipes

Fines Herbes

Fines herbes are equal parts of finely chopped parsley, chives, tarragon, and chervil. Add the fresh herbs to an omelet. Or mix them together with butter for use on potatoes or other fresh vegetables.

Bouquet Garni

Bouquet Garni is whole sprigs of parsley, thyme, and bay leaves tied together, added to flavor soups or stews, and then removed before serving. Other herbs or vegetables may be added, depending on the dish.

Basic Basil Pesto

I prefer extra Parmesan in my pesto, but it can be reduced to two tablespoons. For extra zing, add a pinch of red pepper.

> **1 cup fresh basil leaves, stems removed, washed and dried**
> **2 tablespoons olive oil**
> **2 tablespoons pine nuts**
> **2 cloves of garlic, peeled**
> **¼ cup Parmesan cheese**

Place all ingredients in a blender and blend until the basil is finely chopped. Serve on hot pasta. Or use as a marinade for meat or vegetables.

Pesto with Parsley

This is a less potent pesto.

> **½ cup fresh basil leaves, stems removed, washed and dried**
> **½ cup parsley, stems removed, washed and dried**
> **2 tablespoons olive oil**
> **2 tablespoons pine nuts**
> **¼ cup Parmesan cheese**

Place all ingredients in a blender and blend until the basil is finely chopped. Serve on hot pasta. Or use as a marinade for meat or vegetables.

Lemon Basil Marinade

> **½ cup lemon juice**
> **2 tablespoons olive oil**
> **½ cup lemon basil leaves**
> **dash of pepper**

Combine all ingredients. Pour over chicken or fish and marinate for at least one half hour. Cook the meat thoroughly, discarding the used marinade.

Cilantro Sauce

This is good if you love cilantro. Try substituting the cilantro with basil.

> **1 tablespoon olive oil**
> **½ onion, chopped**
> **1 clove garlic, chopped**
> **4-5 plum tomatoes**
> **tomato paste (optional)**
> **1 cup cilantro, chopped**

Cook the onion in the olive oil until translucent. Add the garlic and cook one minute more. Add the tomatoes and simmer for about five minutes. If the tomatoes are juicy, add tomato paste to thicken the sauce. Before serving, add the cilantro.

Flower Salad

Serve this at the next get-together and see which brave guests eat the flowers

> **Red and green lettuces**
> **Your favorite salad dressing**
> **Flowers: Chive blossoms, calendula flowers,**
> **nasturtium flowers and/or leaves,**
> **pansies — single flowers or combinations**

Arrange lettuces tossed with salad dressing on a plate. Place the flowers on the top.

Herbed Butter

There are many variations on this theme, all of them delicious. Substitute any herb for the tarragon and chervil. The parsley adds color, but it can be removed.

> **¼ cup butter (1/2 stick), room temperature**
> **1 tablespoon parsley, finely chopped**
> **½ tablespoon tarragon, finely chopped**
> **½ tablespoon chervil, finely chopped**

Mix the herbs into the softened butter. For best results, serve on warm, fresh bread (I am hungry already!).

Rosemary and Sage Bread

Trying to keep this as easy as possible, this recipe makes a 1½ lb loaf in the bread machine using the whole-wheat setting. This version is mild: double the herbs for more flavor.

> **Following the directions for the bread**
> **machine, add:**
> **8-9 oz water**
> **2 tablespoons olive oil**
> **1 teaspoon salt**
> **1 tablespoon sugar**
> **1 tablespoon fresh rosemary (1 teaspoon dried)**
> **1 tablespoon fresh sage (1 teaspoon dried)**
> **3 cups whole wheat bread flour**
> **2 teaspoons yeast**

Tarragon Stew

1 boneless, skinless chicken breast,
cut into pieces
1 tablespoon olive oil
1 onion, sliced
1 clove garlic, sliced
2 potatoes, cubed
1 cup chicken broth
½ cup sprigs of fresh tarragon

In a large pan, brown the chicken in the oil. Add the onion and cook until translucent. Add the garlic, potatoes, broth, and tarragon. Cook until the chicken is no longer pink and the potatoes are tender. Serves 2.

Utimate Flu-Fighting Chicken Noodle Soup

1 tablespoon olive oil
1 onion, chopped
2 cloves garlic, chopped
(braver souls may add more)
4 cups chicken broth
2 cups chopped carrots
2 cups cooked chicken, cut into
bite-sized pieces
2 cups wide egg noodles
1 tablespoon fresh thyme
1 tablespoon fresh sage
2 tablespoons fresh parsley

In a large pot, cook the onion in the oil until translucent. Add the garlic for one minute. Add the rest of the ingredients and simmer until the noodles are cooked. Serves 4.

Quick Herb Rolls

These are quick and tasty, fresh from the oven. If you prefer a less-grainy texture, substitute regular flour for the whole wheat flour.

1 cup whole wheat flour
1 cup unbleached flour
4 teaspoons baking powder
2 tablespoons sugar
1 cup skim milk
1 tablespoon chopped fresh herbs
(chives work well)
¼ cup plain yogurt

Preheat the oven to 350° F. Spray a muffin pan with non-stick cooking spray. Mix the dry ingredients together and then add the wet ones. Evenly divide the batter into the 12 muffin tins and bake for 12 minutes, until golden brown. Serve warm.

See Also

Many of the recipes in this book use herbs, which add great flavor, instead of fat and salt.

Asparagus: Asparagus Pasta with Pecans

Beans: Green Bean Casserole, Oregano Green Beans, Italian Chicken Soup

Beets: Vegetable Borscht

Broccoli: Broccoli Soup

Corn: Sweet Corn Soup, Mexican Chicken Soup

Cucumber: Cucumber Salad

Eggplant: Stuffed Eggplant, Veggie Lasagna

Lettuce and greens: Italian Style Vinaigrette, Baked Spinach and Cheese Omelet

Peas: Sweet Green Pea Soup

Peppers: salsas

Potatoes: Picnic Potato Salad, Herbed New Potatoes, Potato Soup

Tomatoes: Italian Tomato Toss, Easy Marinara Sauce, Oven Roasted Tomatoes, Fresh Tomatoes and Mozzarella

Sweet Potatoes: Sweet Potato Soup

Medicinal Herbs

Herbs that are used as medicine are just that—medicine. They are less potent than over-the-counter drugs, but they still have side effects. Overuse of an herb can make a person sick. And some people may have allergies to the plants. Children and pregnant or nursing mothers may want to avoid herbs. The rest of us, especially people already on medication, should consult a doctor before using herbs. Be cautious. That said, the herbs you grow yourself have the advantage of being organic. Also, you know what the herb is and how much of it you are using, as compared to herbs that may or may not be in the supplements in the stores.

Anise

Use this herb to attract butterflies to the garden.

Planting: This herb is best grown in well-drained soil and may be grown in a pot as well. Use seeds or transplants when the ground is warm.

Harvesting: Harvest the seeds when they turn brown. Clip the complete flower heads into a paper bag. Spread out the seeds to dry in a cool, dark place.

Preparing: For a licorice-flavored tea, add 8 oz. boiling water to one teaspoon crushed seeds. Dry leaves can be used, too. And the dry leaves can be used for potpourri as well.

A Healthy Dose: Anise has been used for coughs and to help digestion. Limit to three cups of tea a day.

Bee Balm

Bee balm, also known as Monarda or bergamot, attracts many bees to its brilliant flowers, which range from red to pink to lavendar.

Planting: While it may be grown from seed, the gardener will have better luck with a plant from the nursery. Plant strategically; this plant can be invasive.

Harvesting: Collect the leaves and flowers. Bee balm can be dried for potpourri.

A Healthy Dose: Traditionally used as a tea for digestive ailments, or steamed and inhaled for respiratory ailments.

Borage

Borage has tiny purple flowers, which can be eaten. The leaves taste similar to cucumber.

Planting: Borage can be planted by seed, but is probably best started indoors and then transplanted.

Harvesting: Harvest the young leaves and flowers for fresh eating. The roots and dried seeds can be stored for later uses.

A Healthy Dose: Borage may be a stimulant and has been used to help milk production in nursing mothers (for this use only under the recommendation of a physician).

Calendula

Calendula is also called pot marigold and comes in a wide array of pretty yellows and oranges.

Planting: This flower is best grown in well-drained soil and may be grown in a pot as well. Seeds may be used, but the plants will flower earlier with transplants when the ground is warm.

Preparing: Calendula flowers may be used as an edible garnish.

A Healthy Dose: Calendula is used as a topical antiseptic for the skin. It's best to buy the prepared ointment at the health food store.

Catnip

Cats really do like catnip, so plant it in a protected place, unless it is grown specifically for feline friends.

Planting: Plant by seed or transplant.

Harvesting: Harvest the leaves fresh for tea, or dry them for later uses.

Preparing: Use hot, not boiling, water for catnip tea.

A Healthy Dose: Catnip has been used for menstrual cramps and for digestive problems. Since catnip has a reputation for a natural sedative, use with caution.

Chamomile

Roman chamomile grows about 4 inches tall, while the German grows about 15 inches tall. I use the German variety, which is a fragrant addition to my garden. Chamomile is pretty enough to be grown just for its flowers. Note: People with allergies to ragweed may have a similar reaction to chamomile.

Planting: Chamomile seeds need light to germinate. Lightly scratch the seeds into the soil. Plants can often be found in garden centers. Chamomile often seeds itself, so don't be surprised to see volunteer plants the next year.

Harvesting: Chamomile is ready to harvest when the white petals have pulled back from the yellow center, looking like a badminton birdie. Gently pull the entire flower head from the plant.

Preparing: For tea, pour one cup boiling water over one tablespoon fresh chamomile (or one teaspoon dried).

Storing: Lay the flower heads in a cool, dry, dark space until completely dried. Store the completely dried flower heads in a container out of direct sunlight.

Helpful Hint: Deadhead frequently and the plant should keep flowering.

A Healthy Dose: Chamomile tea is often used a "nighttime tea" to help a person relax before bed. It may also help digestion. Limit to three cups a day. Try chamomile for a hair rinse. Add a small cloth bag of chamomile flowers under hot running water for a scented bath.

Echinacea

Purple Coneflower (Echinacea August-folia) is a lovely native plant that attracts butterflies and hummingbirds with its flowers and American Goldfinches with its seeds.

Planting: Planting seeds in the spring in Minnesota may not result in flowers the first year, but this plant is a perennial. This native prairie flower is best grown in well-drained soil.

Preparing: The roots of the plants are used for medicine, but it's best to buy the already prepared formulas at the store.

A Healthy Dose: Echinacea is best known as a cold and flu remedy.

Feverfew

Both powerful and pretty, feverfew has small flowers with lacy leaves.

Planting: This herb is best grown in well-drained soil and may be grown in a pot as well.

Preparing: The fresh leaves are used; freeze the leaves whole for use in the future. I recommend using the already prepared medicine found in stores.

A Healthy Dose: Originally feverfew was used for fevers. Overseas, feverfew is a popular remedy for migraine headaches. It must be taken every day. Caution: chewing this bitter herb may create sores in your mouth.

Horehound

Horehound lozenges are traditional cough drops.

Planting: Plant horehound with seeds (transplants work, too, of course). It does well in poor soil but doesn't like over-watering.

Harvesting: Clip leaves when needed.

Preparing: Use one teaspoon of dried leaves for 1 cup of boiling water. Use honey or sugar to sweeten.

A Healthy Dose: Horehound repor-tedly helps soothe throats and diminish cough and cold symptoms.

Hyssop

This strong-smelling herb makes an appearance in the Bible.

Planting: Check to make sure you are planting Hyssop officinalis; some other plants share the name but may be harmful when eaten. Use seeds or transplants.

Harvesting: Harvest the leaves as needed. The flowers can also be used.

Preparing: For a cough remedy, use two teaspoons of dried leaves for a cup of boiling water. Use honey to sweeten it.

A Healthy Dose: Hyssop has antiseptic properties, which have been used to treat the herpes virus, as well as expectorant qualities.

Lavender

Ladies used lavender sachets to freshen their clothes in the days before drier sheets.

Planting: Lavender is a perennial in Zone 5, so it may survive a mild winter here in Minnesota, but prepare to re-plant it each year. Since our growing season is short, use transplants so that the plant has enough time to flower.

Harvesting: The spikes of flowers are used for their scent in potpourris and dried for flower arrangements.

A Healthy Dose: Lavender may be good for the skin, so try soaking in a warm tub with lavender.

Lemon Balm

Lemon balm, also called balm or melissa, has a delightful aroma and supposedly keeps away mosquitoes when rubbed on the skin (I've had no such luck).

Planting: This herb should be grown somewhere it can be contained, as it will spread. It may be grown in partial shade. Grow from seed or from plants.

Harvesting: Pick the leaves before or during flowering.

Preparing: Use one tablespoon fresh (dried leaves don't have the same flavor) leaves for one cup of boiling water to make a tea. For a variation, add some of the cooled tea to already-prepared lemonade.

A Healthy Dose: Lemon balm has been used to treat menstrual pain.

Mint

Apple mint, chocolate mint, lemon mint, spearmint, peppermint…the list goes on. These are fun to try and have the added bonus of keeping some pests away.

Planting: This herb probably should be grown in a pot since it really likes to spread. Water these plants well. When searching for a specific kind, buy plants since seeds aren't reliable in producing a certain variety.

Harvesting: Clip leaves almost anytime. Dry in cool, dark spot.

Preparing: Use one tablespoon fresh leaves (one teaspoon dried) for one cup of boiling water to make a tea.

A Healthy Dose: Mint has been used to relieve upset stomachs, nasal congestion, menstrual pain, and headaches.

Nasturtium

Nasturtium colors cover the range of yellow, orange and red. Some are bush types (Jewel), while others trail. Alaska has variegated foliage.

Planting: These are easily planted by seed. The trailing types of nasturtiums may be planted in window boxes or pots for a pretty effect.

Harvesting: Both the flowers and the leaves are used in salads.

Preparing: For a sparkling garnish, dip a slightly damp flower into sugar.

Valerian

Valerian has a pretty, sweet-smelling flower and a reputation as pain-killer and sedative.

Planting: Valerian may be grown from seed. Cats may like this plant as much as catnip, so plant in a place safe from them.

Harvesting: The strong-smelling root is harvested.

A Healthy Dose: Valerian is a strong sedative, traditionally used for a wide variety of ailments. Caution: This plant may be addictive.

Wild
Things

Currently, I have the good fortune to live in relatively undisturbed woods in Minnesota, which contain a plethora of wild plants. One of my favorites is the wild rose, which has delicate pink flowers followed by bright red rose hips in the autumn. I don't even mind that it is taking over my compost corner. The wild fruits and nuts are usually eaten by birds and squirrels, who are quicker than I am, though I can find an occasional leftover.

All of the following can be cultivated, so please take some precautions and care when searching in the wild.

Have permission from the landowner to explore the field or woods in which you are interested. Once exploring, be careful for poison ivy and ticks. Mosquitoes and bees or wasps could be a problem as well. Try dressing in long sleeves and tucking pants into your socks. If any uncertainty remains as to whether or not the plants found are the correct ones, do not eat them. There are poisonous look-alikes.

Depending on the time of year, that fascinating ditch filled with berries could have just been sprayed with potent herbicides. State parks and other public places ask that we take nothing in order to preserve the wild for future generations. In other words, take the time to research the area you want to explore.

If you choose to grow your own versions of these plants, visit a knowledgeable nursery or ask for seeds or cuttings from someone already growing the plant. Do not dig the plants from the wild. Local nurseries will carry the varieties that grow best in your area.

Black Walnut

This beautiful tree can be planted off by itself in your yard because it emits a substance called jugalone, which inhibits the growth of some plants (apples, blackberries, blueberries, tomatoes, to name a few) and the husks leave a dark stain. Its wood is highly valued.

Harvesting: The walnuts are covered in a green "skin" or husk that houses the nut inside. This will stain your fingers. Remove the husks (try driving over them in your car), and then let the shells dry after washing them. The shells are hard (try a hammer).

Preparing: Eat the walnuts fresh or add them to your favorite nut recipes.

A Healthy Dose: One tablespoon of black walnuts contains 46 calories and 4 grams of fat (only .28 saturated fat) as well as 1.3 mcg selenium.

Chokecherries

When we visited my grandmother as children, my brother would spread an inch of chokecherry jelly on his bread, folding the bread and slurping the jelly. The fruits are tart and grow on bushes.

Harvesting: Look for small, dark reddish-black "cherries" sometime in August.

Preparing: Poison alert: Don't eat the pits or the leaves, which contain small amounts of cyanide (hydrocyanic acid). Instead of crushing the berries, make juice by boiling the berries and then straining to remove the pits and skins.

Crab Apples

Some hybrids varieties are meant for ornamentation, but the crab apple is tart and tasty fruit.

Harvesting: Look for ripe fruits in the late summer and throughout the fall.

Preparing: Most crab apples need cooking and sugar. Use crab apples in place of apples in any recipe that calls for tart apples.

A Healthy Dose: One cup of slices has 86 calories as well as 19.8 mg of calcium and 213 mg of potassium.

Cranberries

When we think of cranberries, we think of New England, but Minnesotans can grow this bog-loving berry as well. The traditional cranberry grows on a vine. Highbush cranberry, not a real cranberry, is more likely to be found in Minnesota. Highbush cranberries are, like the name states, bushes.

Harvesting: The almost-ripe white cranberries can be harvested as well as the ripe red ones. Highbush cranberries ripen in September.

Preparing: Both of these fruits need sugar, and highbush cranberries need cooking, too. They are interchangeable in recipes, though the highbush cranberries need straining because of their seeds.

Historical Notes: Cranberries are native to North American and were originally called "craneberries" by Pilgrims.

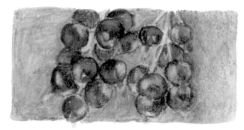

Currants and Gooseberries

Currants can be dried like raisins as well as used fresh. Gooseberries are the prickly version, with thorny stems and fruit. Gooseberries grow wild in the shade of our woods.

Warning: If you decide to grow these, buy plants from a reputable grower to make sure the variety does not carry white pine blister rust.

Harvesting: Look for black currants in August and red currants a bit later. Wild gooseberries ripen in August and are purple.

Preparing: These sour fruits can be eaten straight from the plants, but are better cooked and sweetened.

A Healthy Dose: One cup of red currants has 63 calories and 4.8 grams of fiber as well as 36 mg of calcium and 46 mg of vitamin C.

Dandelion

Yes, dandelion. Try the European salad varieties found in garden catalogs. People with lawns know that dandelions can grow anywhere. Pop off the flower head to avoid spreading the seeds if neighbors are worried.

Harvesting: For tender salad greens, harvest the plant when the leaves are small and young, before the flower has emerged. Dandelion leaves get bitter as they get bigger. Supposedly, the roots can be used as a coffee substitute.

Preparing: Use organic plants. Clip the leaves, rinse, and eat. It's best when added to other greens.

A Healthy Dose: One cup of chopped dandelion greens has 25 calories and 2 grams of fiber as well as 102 mg of calcium and 7700 IU of vitamin A. Dandelion has been used as a diuretic. Be careful: Dandelion may cause allergic reactions.

Elderberries

The blue-black berries of the American elderberry (illustrated above), ripen in late summer, and have been used to make wine and preserves. Poison alert: Eat only the ripe berries—other parts of the plant are poisonous. Also, the bright red berries of the Red or Scarlet elderberry, which ripen earlier in the summer, are poisonous. Be certain what you are picking in the wild.

Harvesting: Elderberries ripen in September. The clustering, purple berries contain three seeds.

Preparing: It's best to add sugar and another tart fruit with elderberries because of their mild taste.

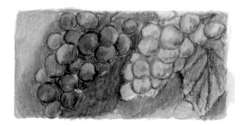

Fiddlehead Ferns

Fiddleheads are the coiled ferns sprouting early in the spring. Cinnamon, bracken, and ostrich ferns are edible.

Harvesting: Harvest as soon as the ferns sprout in spring, while the ferns are tightly coiled.

Preparing: Clean the ferns by removing the hairs. Rinse. Blanch them by placing in boiling water for one minute, removing them, and immediately cooling them in a bowl of ice water. For serving them cold, refrigerate. For serving them warm, boil in fresh water until tender. Bracken ferns may take longer to cook. If you feel daunted by all these steps, some restaurants are serving them and you might even be able to find them in a can.

A Healthy Dose: One hundred grams of fiddlehead ferns has 34 calories, 32 mg of calcium and 29 mg of magnesium.

Grapes

Of course, some gardeners have the expertise and patience to plant cultivated grapes. If you can get wild grapes before the raccoons, you have the sour treat with none of the work.

Harvesting: Look for dark blue grapes in September and October. They'll be smaller and more sour than the ones in the store.

Preparing: These grapes can be eaten fresh or used in jelly.

Hawthorn

Hawthorn trees have pretty red fruits called haws and thorns up and down the trunk and branches. I look forward to our wild hawthorn's blooming every spring, and the bright haws are pretty in the winter.

Harvesting: Look for the ripe haws beginning in September.

Preparing: You could eat these fruits, which look like little apples, but they are best in jams and jellies.

Hazelnuts

We have wild hazelnuts growing on the edges of our woods. The wild nuts are smaller than what you'll find in the grocery stores.

Harvesting: Hazelnuts (or filberts) grow in husks clustered on the bushes and are ready to pick when the nut is easily plucked from the husk.

Preparing: Let the picked nuts dry until crunchy. Eat fresh, add to a salad, or use in your favorite nut recipes.

A Healthy Dose: Ten nuts have 88 calories, 1.3 grams of fiber, and 8.5 grams of fat (only .6 saturated) as well as 16 mg of calcium and 29 mg of magnesium.

Juneberries

Juneberry pie is a favorite of my North Dakota in-laws. Juneberries seem to be a favorite among wild animals, not including the in-laws, of course.

Harvesting: Like the name, Juneberries (or serviceberries or Saskatoon) ripen in June and resemble blueberries. They should taste sweet when they are ready to pick.

Preparing: Use juneberries in recipes just as you would blueberries and other berries.

Lambs' Quarters

Lambs' quarters is also called pigweed, goosefoot, and wild spinach and has a reputation for growing like a weed.

Harvesting: Use the young plants, as the taller they get, the tougher they get.

Preparing: Remove the leaves from the stalk and wash well. Use the leaves like spinach in recipes.

A Healthy Dose: One cup of cooked lambs' quarters has 58 calories and 3.7 grams of fiber as well as 464 mg of calcium and 66 mg of vitamin C.

Nettle

Not surprisingly, this plant contains skin-stinging formic acid, but it disappears with cooking or drying. If you want to plant some, seeds work fine. Use gloves if working with transplants or weeding around this plant.

Harvesting: Use gloves! Harvest the top (and more tender) leaves as needed.

Preparing: Try steaming the nettles in a covered pot for 15 minutes, which should cook away the formic acid.

A Healthy Dose: This spring vegetable is high in vitamins A and C.

Plantain

Plantain is a wild plant; some may call it a weed. It grows prolifically in the lawn and on our gravel driveway.

Preparing: Once the identity of the plant is certain, pick a leaf and crush it against a sore, like a blister, for relief of pain.

A Healthy Dose: This plant has been used for ointments, gargling, eyewashes, constipation and diarrhea.

Plums

The native American plum is cold hardy and has been used to develop some hybrids such as La Crescent. The wild fruits are smaller than the hybrids.

Harvesting: Plums will fall of the branches easily when they are ripe. Look for them in September.

Preparing: Just wash and eat these delicious fruits. Poison Alert: Do not eat the pits.

A Healthy Dose: One plum has 36 calories and one gram of fiber as well as 114 milligrams of potassium and 213 IU of vitamin A.

Red Clover

This grows wild at the edges of our yard, which of course has yet to see an herbicide. Red clover can be grown relatively easily from seed.

Harvesting: Pick the flowers at their peak. They may be used fresh or dried.

Preparing: Use one teaspoon dried flowers for each cup of boiling water.

A Healthy Dose: This plant may contain an estrogen-like chemical and has been used to treat menopausal symptoms.

Rose

I can't say enough about the wild rose, which grows near our garden. During the time it blossoms, driving on the county road, I can see bright pink blossoms of other wild roses growing near the ditches.

Planting: Some people grow hybridized and cultivated versions of the wild rose. The wild rose has a short but beautiful display of flowers, and the fragrance is subtle yet spinningly intoxicating.

Harvesting: Rose petals may be eaten. For rose hips, do not pick the blossoms. Rose hips are the fruit that follows the flower. After the first frost, the hips may be harvested. Rose hips are high in vitamin C.

Preparing: Rose hips are tart and are good for jelly.

Wood Sorrel

I see rabbits nibbling at the patches of wood sorrel, which grow wild in our yard.

Harvesting: Poison alert: This plant contains small amounts of oxalic acid, which can be poisonous when ingested in large quantities. Pick pesticide-free leaves as needed.

Preparing: I suggest adding just a few leaves to a salad for a sour burst.

A Healthy Dose: Wood sorrel is high in vitamin C.

Yarrow

Yarrow is a native perennial with clusters of tiny flowers and feathery, ferny leaves. Achillea hybrids grow in soft pastel colors for the garden but have white flowers in the wild.

Planting: Yarrow may be grown from seed or plants. It likes well-drained soil and sun.

A Healthy Dose: Yarrow has been used to treat wounds and as a sedative.

Recipes

Easy Fruit Jam

—no canning required
As a youngster, I watched my grandmother cook strawberry jam on the stove. She didn't even measure, stirring the fruit until it thickened. And it was so amazingly good that we couldn't even wait for it to cool before we ate it. She didn't have time to can it before it was gone. I've tried to make jam her way and this is the closest I could get.

> **1 cup mashed fruit**
> **1 cup bite-size fruit**
> **1 cup sugar**

Bring the mashed fruit and the sugar to a boil, stirring constantly. Add the second cup and fruit and heat through. Store in an air-tight container in the refrigerator for up to two weeks.

Easy Fruit Jelly

—no canning required
Create fruit juice from wild fruits by mashing and straining. With chokecherries, be careful not to crush the pits. Follow the directions on the pectin package because they differ from brand to brand.

> **fruit juice**
> **sugar**
> **pectin**
> **lemon juice**

Prepare according to the pectin directions. Store in an air-tight container in the refrigerator for up to two weeks.

Cranberry Sauce

> **2 cups cranberries**
> **1 cup orange juice**
> **1 cup sugar**
> **grated peel of one orange**

Bring the juice and sugar to a boil and stir to dissolve the sugar. Add the cranberries and the orange peel and simmer ten minutes, stirring frequently.

Fruit Pie

I am not above buying pre-made crusts, especially when I like to focus on the filling of the pie anyway. When you'd like to make your own, this is a good recipe.

Pie Crust for a Two Crust Pie

2 cups flour
1 tablespoon sugar
⅔ cup butter
cold water

Cut the butter into the flour and sugar. Add the water one tablespoon at a time until a ball of dough is formed. You might need up to four tablespoons of water. Divide the dough and place it between sheets of waxed paper to avoid a very sticky mess. Roll each part into a circle large enough to fit your pie tin.

Filling

I often cheat on the filling by cramming as much fruit into the crust as I can, which results in a tasty though messy pie. Use this recipe as a guideline. One of my favorites is strawberry rhubarb. Also, I like tarter pies so I usually use less sugar. Feel free to experiment by mixing fruits to make Bumbleberry Pie, as my mother-in-law Marlyne affectionately calls it.

4 cups fruit (bite-sized or sliced,
peeled or pitted, depending
on the fruit)
1 cup sugar (use less sugar if you
feel the fruit is sweet, such
as apples and pears)
¼ cup flour
optional: one tablespoon of
lemon juice for tartness
optional: one teaspoon of
cinnamon
optional: ½ teaspoon nutmeg

Note: Apple pies or pear pies need only two tablespoons of flour. Use extra flour for fruit that has been frozen.

Bake the pie in a 350° F oven until the fruit is tender and the crust is golden brown. If the edges get too dark before the pie is done, cover the edges with aluminum foil.

Flowers

What's a garden without flowers? (As my literal-minded husband would say, "It's a garden without flowers.") Flowers add beauty with their stunning colors and luscious scents.

Most flowers need well-drained soil, regular watering, and planting after the danger of frost has passed. To save money, grow annuals from seed. Perennials may also be grown from seed, though some will not flower until the second year. For instant color that lasts the entire season, use transplants and keep the plant blooming by removing the fading flowers.

Some gardeners like to have separate flower, herb and vegetable gardens. Yet it's often more efficient to combine the different plants. This helps the organic gardener as well, since flowers provide pollen for beneficial insects and smelly herbs keep away some pests. A garden that is full of diversity is less at risk for a pest invasion. I have planted pansies (otherwise known as bunny candy) among some of my herbs and the rabbits leave the flowers alone. Have fun experimenting with different combinations.

This compilation of flowers is not comprehensive, but it includes flowers in our gardens or growing nearby.

Alyssum

Annual
Full sun
Attracts beneficial insects and butterflies
Easy to grow

Alyssum is a low growing annual covered in tiny white blossoms (it also comes in pastel pinks and purples as well).

Planting: Alyssum can be planted from seed, but it flowers more quickly when bought as a plant from the garden center.

Helpful Hint: Alyssum attracts good bugs, so plant it everywhere. It fills in bare spots nicely and makes a good groundcover or border

Aster

Perennial
Full Sun

Asters, best known for their bright flowers, come in a wide range of colors and sizes. Many native plants are members of the aster family, including New England Aster, Large-leaved Aster and Flat-topped Aster. Many other beautiful varieties are available, too. Most asters bloom in the late summer, just when a bit of color is needed.

Planting: Asters need full sun. For seeds, cover lightly and firmly with soil.

Helpful hint: In June, trim the tall growing asters back a bit to encourage the plants to produce more flowers.

Astilbe

Perennial
Partial shade
Easy to grow

Description: Also called false spirea, astilbe has fern-like foliage and feathery flowers, which come in shades of pink and white.

Planting: Use transplants in a partly shady area, for example, an east-facing slope. Even though I forget about my astilbe until they flower, they seem to thrive on their own.

Helpful Hint: Astilbes and hostas can be grown in shady spots together.

Bachelor Button

Annual
Full sun
Easy to grow
Edible flowers

Description: Bachelor Buttons (also called corn flower) are fluffy blue flowers that grow two or three feet tall. They come in white and pastel pink and purple as well.

Planting: Bachelor Buttons can be planted from seed easily. Sometimes they will re-seed themselves for the net year.

Helpful Hint: Bachelor Buttons also attracts beneficial bugs.

Begonia

Annual and tuber
Partial shade
Easy to grow

Description: There are two types of begonia: tuberous begonias and wax begonias. Tuberous begonias grow from tubers and have lush, colorful flowers which look great in containers. Wax begonias are compact plants with delicate, waxy flowers and can be grown as houseplants.

Planting: Wax begonias can be grown from cuttings. For color in the garden, use transplants. They can be planted in partial shade or full sun. Tuberous begonias can grow in partial or full shade. Start the tubers indoors or buy the already started ones in the garden center. In Minnesota, store the tubers indoors during the winter.

Helpful Hint: Tuberous begonias, especially the cascading varieties, look terrific in pots.

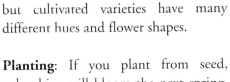

Columbine

Native perennial
Full sun
Attracts hummingbirds

Description: Columbine is a native wildflower often found in woodlands (it grows wild around our place). The native ones are red with yellow centers, but cultivated varieties have many different hues and flower shapes.

Planting: If you plant from seed, columbine will bloom the next spring. These plants need full sun, but can probably tolerate a little shade.

Helpful Hint: Collect the seeds for planting next year or sharing.

Cosmos

Annual
Full sun
Easy to grow

Description: Cosmos is a feathery-foliaged flower ranging in height from 18 to 30 inches, depending on the variety. I personally like Sensation, which grows 4 feet tall with pastel pink, purple, and white flowers. Sonata is the short version, 18 inches tall. For a unique tube-shaped petals, try Sea Shells. Bright Lights is also lovely in red, orange and gold.

Planting: Cosmos can be planted from seed, but it flowers more quickly when transplanted

Helpful Hint: Cosmos looks great in mass plantings.

Crocus

Hardy corms
Full sun
Easy to grow

Description: Crocuses bloom early and beautifully, coming in a wide range of white, yellows and purples with narrow green or variegated leaves. The saffron crocus is the crocus grown for its stamens to make the expensive seasoning.

Planting: Plant in the fall, mulching well, about 6 weeks before the ground freezes, sometime in September or early October, which gives the corms a chance to get their roots ready for winter.

Helpful Hint: If your crocuses are eaten by squirrels (or other digging pests), try planting them in wire or mesh in the ground.

Daffodil

Hardy bulb
Full to partial sun
Resists animal pests
Poisonous

Description: Nothing eats daffodils—not rabbits, not deer, not squirrels. King Alfred is the bright yellow variety, but daffodils also come in a variety of shapes and colors. (Narcissus is the family name, covering narcissi, jonquils and daffodils.)

Planting: Daffodils prefer well-drained soil and full sun, but they may do okay in part shade. Plant the bulbs 6 inches deep about 6 weeks before the ground freezes, to give the bulbs a chance to get their roots ready for winter. Some varieties may require different planting depths. Many kinds of daffodils spread out and keep growing year after year.

Helpful Hint: Pick the flowers when they die so that the plants store their energy in the bulbs, not the seeds.

Daisy

Perennial
Full sun
Attracts butterflies
Easy to grow

Description: Ox-eye daisies are often found growing along roadsides in Minnesota, even though it is not a native wildflower. Some varieties of daisies are bred for bigger blooms. Daisies tend to have floppy stems, but these healthy plants bloom so prolifically in my garden that I can forgive them that minor fault. This is definitely one of my favorites.

Planting: Plant daisies in full sun. They can be grown from seeds. Once daisies find a spot they like, they will spread.

Helpful Hint: Remove the flowers after they have finished blooming so the energy goes to the roots of the plants for better blooms the next year.

Dame's Rocket

Annual or biennial
Full to partial shade
Attracts butterflies and hummingbirds
Easy to grow

Description: Dame's Rocket (also called Dame's Violet) has its roots in Europe, but it grows wild throughout Minnesota. It resembles garden phlox, another beautiful plant for the garden.

Planting: Grow from seed in well-drained soil.

Helpful Hint: Cut the flowers off after blooming to encourage a second bloom.

Foxglove

Biennial
Partial shade
Resists deer
Poisonous

Description: This tall plant has distinctive flowers on spikes. Foxglove is the origin of digitalis (the heart drug), although the plant is poisonous, especially for children.

Planting: Foxglove can be grown from seed and will re-seed itself, too. Since it can grow up to 5 feet tall, depending on the variety, plant these behind shorter flowers.

Helpful Hint: Foxgloves will grow well in sandy soil.

Geranium

Annual
Full sun
Easy to grow
Edible leaves and flowers (scented geranium)

Description: Geraniums' gorgeous flowers and ability to withstand the heat and humidity of Minnesota summers make them a popular plant. Ivy leaf geraniums spread well, making them a good choice as a ground cover or potted plant. Zonal geraniums have a reddish zone circling their leaves; they come in a wide range of colors and are well stocked at the nursery. Variegated geraniums have white-rimmed leaves. Regal geraniums have bi-colored blossoms. Scented geraniums can sometimes grow spindly and have tiny flowers, but the leaves have bewitching scents: lemon, rose, chocolate mint, and more.

Planting: While some geraniums do grow from seed, garden centers have a wide array of plants to choose from. Geraniums will do well in full sun and can tolerate a bit of shade, too. Geraniums do well in sunny windows, so pot up and bring inside your favorites to brighten falls' frosty days.

Helpful Hint: Garnish lemonade with lemon-scented geranium leaves, add rose-scented leaves to apple jelly recipes, or top cakes with scented leaves and blossoms.

Golden Glow

Native perennial
Full sun
Attracts butterflies

Description: Golden Glow is also called Green-headed Coneflower. This tall plant (up to 8 feet) makes an impressive display with its abundant bright flowers.

Planting: Golden Glow grows in moist soil; its original habitat is prairies. Since it grows so tall, plant it where it won't shade other plants in your garden.

Helpful Hint: For the wild plant enthusiast, many garden centers now carry native plants, which have been grown from seed.

Hosta

Perennial
Shade
Easy to grow

Description: Not everyone has a sunny spot for a garden. Hostas are a wonderful shade plant with striking foliage ranging from spears to heart-shapes and leaves of blue to green and variegated with white. Their spikes of flowers are pretty but short-lived, so I suggest planting with impatiens for color.

Planting: Buy the plants from a nursery. Water hostas well, especially in the fall. Once established, it's easy to divide the roots for planting in other parts of your garden.

Helpful Hint: If slugs are a problem, take a used margarine container, press it into the soil, and fill it with stale beer (yeast mixed with sugar water also works). Slugs will drown after trying to drink that tasty brew.

Impatiens

Annual
Shade
Easy to grow
Edible flower

Description: Impatiens add a burst of color in shady spots. They spread nicely and are easy to grow. You'll have a wide variety of choices of these popular plants: single impatiens with pastel colors and orange and burgundy, double impatiens blossoms that look like roses, and New Guinea impatiens, the more sun tolerant of the bunch.

Planting: Buy these annual plants from the garden center and plant them in shade.

Helpful Hint: Another colorful choice for shady areas is coleus, with its red, green, and variegated foliage.

Iris

Perennial
Full sun
Easy to grow
Poisonous

Description: In Greek mythology, Iris is the goddess of the rainbow, so it is a fitting name for this flower, since irises come in many colors besides the familiar purples. Bearded irises are the traditional irises, with full flowers and impressive spring colors. Siberian irises have more delicate flowers than the bearded and require damper soil.

Planting: Irises are surprising easy to grow. Plant the rhizomes in late summer or early fall. Cut the flower stalks off after blooming. In late summer, cut the leaves back to 3 or 4 inches (a fan shape looks pretty). Mulch well for winter. Every few years dig up the rhizomes and cut away the woody parts, separating the healthy parts into new plants. In fact, it's pretty easy to find people willing to give away some irises in August.

Helpful Hint: Are your irises not blooming? They could be planted too deeply; plant them just below the soil level.

Lady's Slipper

Native perennial
Shade

Description: According to Stan Tekiela in *Wildflowers of Minnesota,* there are 42 native orchids growing in Minnesota, including Yellow Lady's Slipper and our state flower Showy Lady's Slipper.

Planting: Lady's slippers do not transplant well, requiring wet conditions and a special fungus that helps them grow. It's best to enjoy these plants just where they are. Do not dig them from the wild.

Helpful Hint: Some lady's slippers take 20 years before they bloom. Find their distinctive foliage and then watch for the flowers beginning in early summer.

Lily

Perennial and hardy bulbs
Full sun and partial sun
Easy to grow

Description: Lilies are easy to plant but are stunningly colorful. They come in just about every shape and size to fit your garden. Asiatic lilies bloom before oriental lilies. Hardy and fast-growing daylilies, named because a blossom lasts only a day, can be grown in part-shade and are easily divided to be shared with neighbors (Stella D'oro is a popular variety). Note: most lilies cannot be eaten. Daylilies may be a laxative.

Planting: Lilies can be planted in the spring, but may do better when planted in the fall in well-drained soil. Plant the basic bulbs 6 inches deep in full sun in the fall, about 6 weeks before the ground freezes, sometime in September or early October. Some varieties may require different planting depths. Many kinds of lilies naturalize (spread out and keep growing year after year).

Helpful Hint: Cut off the stamens of the lilies before bringing them into your home since the bright yellow pollen stains clothing (and just about anything else it touches).

Marigold

Annual
Full sun
Repels nematodes
Easy to grow
Edible flowers

Description: Marigolds are a colorful, easy, and helpful annual. Folklore says rabbits stay away from their smell, and the plants may repel nematodes. Garden centers carry many colors and varieties of this popular plant. The plants range from 10 inches to almost 4 feet, and the colors range from creamy white to deep rust with just about very shade of yellow and orange in between. The flowers may be small or extra large. Experiment with and enjoy this flower!

Planting: Plant marigolds in full sun. For seeds, cover lightly and firmly with soil. They will grow quickly, but if a gardener wants instant color, plant transplants after the chance of frost.

Helpful Hint: Popping off the dead flower heads will prolong the life of marigold plants.

Milkweed

Native perennial
Sun to shade
Attracts butterflies
Poisonous

Description: Milkweed is named because of its milky sap. Monarch butterflies lay their eggs on milkweed plants, making it an essential plant to the butterflies' survival.

Planting: Milkweed is a versatile plant and should grow well in most gardens.

Helpful Hint: If you are growing milkweed to attract Monarch butterflies, plan on letting the caterpillars munch their way through the leaves. Then watch for the chrysalises, and later the emerging butterflies.

Morning Glory

Annual vine
Full sun
Easy to grow
Poisonous

Description: Morning Glories are annual vines with trumpet like flowers that open only in the morning. They come in white, pink, blue, and lavender. They self-seed profusely. In fact, the seeds I grow each year are saved from the plants that grew in my parents' garden…which they never planted. (I'm guessing the previous owner or an industrious bird did the original planting.)

Planting: Plant morning glories in full sun. Cover the seeds lightly and firmly with soil.

Helpful Hint: Soak the seeds overnight for quicker germination.

Peony

Perennial
Full to partial sun
Easy to grow

Description: These large, colorful and beautifully scented flowers have perfect timing, blooming as the tulips are fading. Single and double blossoms are available in variations of red, pink and white.

Planting: Plant peonies in what will be their permanent spot, placing the eyes 2 inches below the surface...too deep and the plant won't flower well, too shallow and frost may kill it. Once planted, peonies will continue to bloom year after year.

Helpful Hint: The large flowers will need staking so they don't flop over in the wind or after a heavy rain. Place a wire cage or stakes threaded with string over the peony before it grows. Or stake the individual flowers a needed.

Spiderwort

Native perennial
Full sun

Description: Spiderwort has lovely spring flowers, which bloom in the mornings, and stems that look like grass.

Planting: Spiderwort prefers well-drained soil. Since the clusters of flowers open one at a time, spiderwort looks best planted together in groups.

Helpful Hint: Be careful when weeding; emerging spiderwort looks like grass.

Sunflower

Native annual
Full sun
Attracts birds
Easy to grow
Edible flower petals and seeds

Description: The common sunflower is a native plant, and it has been bred for special uses, everything from food to flowers. Usually we think of sunflowers as large plants, but some varieties are compact and pretty, made especially for cutting.

Planting: Plant the seeds early, as soon as the soil can be worked, about ½ inch deep, about 3-4 seeds per foot, thinning to one plant every 18 inches or so (depending on the variety). Sunflowers, as their name implies, like full sun.

Helpful Hint: Leave the flower head on the plant to dry, and watch the birds feast!

Tulips

Hardy bulb
Full sun

Description: Tulips certainly are versatile, some blooming early on the spring, other varieties blooming later. They vary in height from 3 to 15 inches and in color, too, from deep colors like red to pastels.

Planting: Plant tulips in the fall, before the ground freezes. Animals like to eat tulip bulbs, so plant them in a wire cage or protected location. Tulips can be planted like annuals for cut flowers. While tulips will come back year after year, they will be smaller than when they were first planted and some may require re-planting after a couple of years.

Helpful Hint: Plant the bulbs in the ground three times the height of the bulb.

Viola

Annual
Full sun
Easy to grow
Edible flowers

Description: Viola includes violas, violets, pansies and Johnny-jump-ups. Some violets are native plants; we have purple and yellow wild violets in our woods. Pansies are famous for their "faces," coming in a wide variety of shades and mixtures of colors. The most popular are the purple and yellow varieties. Just this summer I planted delicate blooms of purple, lavender and white.

Planting: Use transplants for instant spring color in full sun. For seeds, cover lightly and firmly with soil. Deadheading helps keep the plants flowering, though they may self-sow if you let them go to seed.

Helpful Hint: Pansies are a cool weather flower.

Water Lily

Native perennial
Full to partial sun

Description: As its names suggests, this plant grows in water. With the White Water Lily and Yellow Water Lily can both we found in lakes and ponds in Minnesota. The American Lotus grows in lakes in southeastern Minnesota.

Planting: The lilies prefers quiet water, as the leaves and flowers float with their roots embedded in the soil beneath. The American lotus grows above the water.

Helpful Hint: With the popularity of water gardens, why not grow a native water lily? Ask for them at a nursery that specializes in water gardens.

Wormwood

Perennial
Full sun
Repels insect pests
Poisonous

Description: Though wormwood has smallish white or yellow flowers, it may repel insect pests in the garden. It grows to twelve inches tall. Wormwood has been used as a healing herb, but since it is a strong herb and may be poisonous, I recommend it only as pest control in the garden.

Planting: While seeds can be used, transplants are a better choice.

Helpful Hint: Plant wormwood where you have previously had problems with flea beetles and slugs. Make a wormwood tea to spray for aphids on fruit trees and other infested plants.

Zinnia

Annual
Full sun
Attracts butterflies
Easy to grow

Description: I remember my grandmother's garden in the late summer when it overflowed with tall, brightly colored zinnias. Those flowers attracted hordes of butterflies year after year. Zinnias grow tall (Cut and Come Again and Oklahoma) and short (Thumbelina and Profusion) in a wide array of colors. Candy Cane has striped petals.

Planting: For seeds, cover lightly and firmly with soil. They will grow quickly, but for instant color, plant transplants after the chance of frost.

Helpful Hint: Plant extras, since zinnias are colorful cut flowers.

Challenges for the Expert Gardener

Do people marvel at the size of your rutabagas? Are they shocked that you plant seeds outside when it's still snowing? Are your south-facing windows crowded with seedlings ready to go outside in the middle of April? You are either crazy or an expert gardener (or both). Chances are you are familiar with seed-starting, seed saving, row covers, plastic mulch, and garden gadgets galore. So this chapter is dedicated to expert gardeners, and hopefully you'll have fun growing these selections in Minnesota's challenging weather.

Hardy Kiwi

Northern hardy kiwis are smoother than their fuzzy southern relations. Kiwis are a bit tricky with pollination. Some plants are male and some are female. The males have to blossom the same time as the females to produce fruit. One trick is to plant more male vines than the recommended one male to eight females or plant the variety Issai, which is self-fertile and hardy in zone 4.

Planting. Kiwis need well drained soil and plenty of mulch. Plant the vines 15 feet apart in a spot protected from frosts, perhaps a south-facing slope. Use sturdy trellises with kiwis, training them up and pruning their vigorous growth. Cover the trucks with burlap for the winter.

Harvesting: Pick the firm fruits when the seeds are black.

Preparing: Peel and eat! Kiwis can also be canned and dried.

Storing: Kiwis will keep in the refrigerator for several weeks, perhaps up to 6 months.

Helpful Hint: Keep a small piece of stem on the kiwi to prolong storage life.

A Healthy Dose: One medium kiwi without its skin has 46 calories and 2.5 grams of fiber as well as 74 mg of vitamin C and 29 mcg of folate.

Historical Notes: Originally called Chinese gooseberry (and not selling well), Freida Caplan re-named it "kiwi fruit" after the kiwi bird of New Zealand.

Recipe

Mini Fruit Pizzas
Sugar cookies
Strawberry flavored cream cheese
Sliced kiwi
Raspberries or sliced strawberries

Spread the cream cheese on a sugar cookie. Arrange the kiwi and berries on top.

Leeks

Leeks have a mild onion taste. The challenge with leeks is their long growing season (130 days) and the blanching required for white stalks. Try Electra or Large American Flag.

Planting: Leeks need to be started indoors since we just don't have 130 days of summery weather in Minnesota. When the transplants are ready, plant them in a trench about 5 or 6 inches deep. Leeks need nourishment (lots of compost). As the leeks grow, fill in an inch every so often around the leeks for blanching.

Harvesting: When the leeks have a ½ inch diameter, you may begin harvesting them, though you may want to leave some in the ground to get bigger.

Preparing: Rinse well and remove the roots. Cut off the tough green leaves. Use as you would onions, though they are much milder. Normally leeks are used only for their white stalks.

Storing: Leeks keep well, wrapped and stored in the fridge.

Helpful Hint: Since leeks get so sandy, sometimes it's best to slice the leek as needed for the recipe and then wash it so that all the grit can be rinsed away.

A Healthy Dose: One fourth of a cup of cooked and chopped leek has 8 calories and 8 mg of calcium.

Historical Notes: In America in the 1800s leeks were sold with parsley for use in soups.

Recipes

Saucy Leeks

> **2 leeks, thinly sliced**
> **2 tablespoons olive oil, divided**
> **1 green onion, chopped**
> **1 tablespoon chopped**
>   **fresh tarragon**
> **½ cup milk**
> **grated lemon peel (optional)**

Sauté the leeks in one tablespoon olive oil. Remove them onto a serving platter. In the same pan, lightly sauté the green onion and tarragon in the second tablesopon of olive oil. Add the milk to heat it. Pour the sauce over the leeks and sprinkle with the lemon peel.

Chicken and Leek Pasta Toss

> **8 ounces pasta, cooked**
> **2 tablespoons olive oil**
> **1 leek, sliced**
> **1 chicken breast, sliced**
> **black pepper to taste**
> **fresh basil, optional**

Cook the chicken breast and the leek in the olive oil. Season with black pepper to taste. Add to the hot pasta. Add basil, if desired.

Mushrooms

Mushrooms come in all shapes and sizes: button, morel, portabella, shiitake, and more. If you plan on searching for them in the wild, take a good field guide with you since some mushrooms are deadly. But if you grow your own, you can be assured of the variety.

Planting: If you've got a dark, humid spot, you can probably grow mushrooms. I often have some sprouting from the old mushroom mulch I place under my plants in the garden. Mushrooms can be grown outdoors, but I'd suggest using a kit, which you can order from garden catalogs.

Preparing: Wipe the mushrooms with a damp cloth, checking for dirt in cracks. Trim any dry or tough spots.

Storing: Mushrooms may last a week in the refrigerator. Fresh mushrooms can be frozen in airtight containers.

Helpful Hint: Mushrooms will absorb water, so avoid soaking them.

A Healthy Dose: One half cup of raw pieces has 9 calories as well as 26 IU of vitamin D and 3 mcg of selenium.

Historical Notes: The Chinese have eaten mushrooms for food as well as medicine for 2500 years.

Recipes

Mushroom and Sweet Pepper Quesadilla

2 large tortillas
1 tablespoon olive oil
½ cup sliced mushrooms
½ cup sliced red pepper
1 cup shredded
pepper jack cheese

In a sauté pan, sauté the mushroom and pepper until tender. On a baking sheet, place one tortilla. Spoon the mushrooms and pepper on top. Cover with cheese. Top with the last tortilla. Bake in a 350° F oven until the cheese melts.

Seitan Soup

This recipe is from Jessie, a most adventurous food taster.

1 tablespoon olive oil
2 onions, chopped
½ cup flour
4 cups vegetable broth
¼ cup shoyu sauce (tamari or
soy sauce can be substituted)
1 cup red wine
1 tablespoon honey
1 tablespoon rice wine vinegar
3 carrots, chopped
4 potatoes, chopped
4 tomatoes, chopped
½ cup morel mushrooms
1 pound seitan (cooked
chicken can be substituted)
2 zucchini, chopped
½ cup parsley, chopped

Brown the onions in the olive oil. Add ¼ cup flour. Slowly add one cup broth. Then add the rest of the broth and all of the ingredients except for the zucchini and the parsley. Simmer until the vegetables are tender. Add the zucchini for the last few minutes of cooking. Stir in the parsley just before serving.

Sautéed Mushrooms

2 tablespoons butter
2 cups sliced mushrooms

In a sauté pan, melt butter (or use olive oil). Add clean, sliced mushrooms and cook until tender, stirring occasionally.

Mac and Cheese with Mushrooms and Peas

1 one pound box of pasta,
cooked and drained
double recipe of cheese sauce
for vegetables (see Brussels
Sprouts)
½ cup sautéed mushrooms
½ cup fresh peas, steamed
1 cup shredded sharp
cheddar cheese

Toss the hot pasta, mushrooms, and peas with the hot cheese sauce. Sprinkle on the extra cheese just before serving.

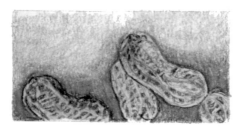

Peanuts

Peanuts can grow in Minnesota. Early Spanish peanut is a smaller but earlier variety than Jumbo Virginia.

Planting: Mound the dirt into a hill and plant the nuts 1–1½ inches deep, 18 inches apart. Mound soil around the plant when they are 12 inches tall. According to William L Nunn, "Soon, lower flower-leaves will fall and slender peduncles appear. These will burrow back into the hills and each will produce a single peanut at its tip." Mulch the plants heavily.

Harvesting: Pull up the plants after frost has killed them, brushing off the extra dirt and hanging the whole plant to dry in a warm place for 8 weeks.

Preparing: Remove the shells and the skins and eat. Or dry roast the shelled and skinned nuts by placing them on a baking sheet and bake in a 350° F oven until toasted and fragrant, watching carefully so they don't burn.

Storing: After the nuts have dried, store them in a cool, dry place.

Helpful Hint: Try warming the soil with plastic mulch and extending the season with row covers.

A Healthy Dose: One ounce of raw Spanish peanuts has 161 calories, 7 grams of protein, 2.7 grams of fiber, and 14 grams of fat (only two are saturated) as well as 30 grams of calcium and 53 milligrams of magnesium.

Historical Notes: In Peru, the Inca grew peanuts in irrigated fields.

Recipes

Chicken Wraps

4 tortillas
1 cup leftover cooked chicken
in bite-sized pieces
4 cups fresh lettuces and greens
1 cup shredded carrots
1 cup chopped peanuts

Divide the ingredients over the four tortillas and roll them like a burrito. If desired, add a dash of bottled taco sauce for extra flavor.

Peanutty Brownie Loaves

1 ⅓ cups semi-sweet
  chocolate chips
6 tablespoons butter
3 large eggs, slightly beaten
1 cup sugar
1 teaspoon vanilla
¾ cup flour
4 tablespoons baking cocoa
⅛ teaspoon baking soda
½ cup chopped peanuts
additional peanuts and chocolate
  chips for garnish, if desired

Grease the bottoms of 8 mini-loaf pans. Melt the chocolate chips and the butter in a microwave safe bowl for 30 seconds, stirring to help melt. (Be careful not to burn the chocolate.) Cool slightly. Stir in the sugar. Add the vanilla and eggs. Carefully stir in the flour, cocoa, and baking soda. Add the peanuts. Evenly divide the batter between the 8 loaf pans. Top with the additional peanuts and chips, if desired. Bake in a 350° F oven for 20 minutes, until the crust on top looks dry. Cool in the pan for a few minutes, and then carefully remove the loaves from their pans to finish cooling.

Homemade Peanut Butter

Food process dry roasted peanuts in small batches. Refrigerate.

Sweet Potatoes

Sweet potatoes are a tropical plant, but they can be grown in Minnesota's hot and humid summers with a short season variety, such as Georgia Jet and Centennial. Porto Rico and Vardaman are compact varieties for smaller gardens.

Planting: Sweet potato transplants can be bought in some nurseries. Or start your own indoors. Dig the soil deeply, with lots of compost. Plant them about 12 inches apart. Water well.

Harvesting: Before a hard frost, dig the sweet potatoes out of the ground. With a pitchfork, loosen the soil around the plants carefully and search. Spread the sweet potatoes out to dry outdoors, removing any soft, broken, or bruised ones, before storing them together. To cure them, keep them in a very warm spot for 10 days.

Preparing: Sweet potatoes are versatile. Bake them in a pan in the oven or microwave. Or fry or mash or puree or simmer.

Storing: Store in a cool, dry place.

Helpful Hint: Try the leaves of the sweet potatoes. One cup chopped has 28 mcg of folate.

A Healthy Dose: One medium baked sweet potato has 117 calories and 3.4 grams of fiber as well as 28 milligrams of vitamin C and 28 mcg of folate.

Historical Notes: The Aztecs grew sweet potatoes, a plant native to the more tropical areas of the Americas.

Recipes

Mashed Sweet Potatoes

This also works with baking potatoes.

3 cups cubed sweet potatoes
1½ cups water or chicken broth
black pepper, to taste
milk, to taste
butter, to taste

Cut the potatoes in the water until tender. Drain the potatoes, reserving the cooking liquid, if desired. Mash them, adding milk and butter until smooth and tasty. For healthier mashed potatoes, use the cooking liquid instead.

Candied Sweet Potatotes

2 cups sweet potatoes,
  already cooked
¼ cup butter
½ cup brown sugar
1 tablespoon milk

Melt the butter in a large pan. Add the rest of the ingredients and cook until hot and bubbly.

Sweet Potato Soup

1 tablespoon olive oil
1 large onion, chopped
½ tablespoon freshly
  grated ginger
1 large sweet potato, cubed
1 cup chicken broth
1 cup milk
¼ cup chopped chives

Cook the onion in the olive oil until translucent. Add the ginger, the sweet potato, and the chicken broth. Simmer until the potato is tender. Stir in the milk and cook just until heated. Sprinkle with the chives.

Sweet Potato Chips

This also works for other potatoes… even eggplant! Combine the veggies for a festive platter.

2 sweet potatoes
oil for frying
salt, pepper, or chili powder
  to taste

Peel the sweet potatoes. Slice them thinly. In a deep pan, heat the oil. Add a few slices at a time, cooking until golden. Remove carefully (try a slotted spoon) and drain on paper towels. Repeat with the remaining slices. Season the chips and serve hot.

See Also

Brussels Sprouts: Brussels Sprout
  Soup
Celery: Blasted Veggie Soup
Rutabaga: Roasted Root Vegetables

Helpful Resources

Websites

These websites may have useful information (though many are just trying to sell you something), but some of the seed catalog sites are even better (such as seedsavers.org).

gardening.about.com
Type in "organic gardening" in the search feature and you'll find lots of information.

www.marthastewart.com
This site encourages you to buy their products, but gardening and cooking are two of Martha's specialties.

www.organicgardening.com
This one encourages magazine subscriptions, of course, but the information is useful.

www.rebeccasgarden.com
This is based on the TV show and has some nice ideas and pictures.

www.nal.usda.gov
The information about calories and nutrients in this book comes from this web site.

Catalogs

I recommend buying plants from the garden center (so you can see what you are getting), but the garden catalogs are fun to browse and often have unusual seed varieties that can't be found in stores. The following catalogs are free.

Burpee
W. Atlee Burpee & Co.
300 Park Avenue
Warminster PA 18991-0001
1-800-888-1447
www.burpee.com

The Cooks Garden
P. O. Box 535
Londonderry VT 05148
1-800-457-9703
cooksgarden.com

Garden's Alive (organic garden products including fertilizer)
5100 Schenley Place
Lawrenceburg IN 47025
(812) 537-8650
www.GardensAlive.com

Johnny's Selected Seeds
Foss Hill road
Albion ME
(207) 437-4301
www.johnnyseeds.com

Park Seed Co.
1 Parkton Avenue
Greenwood SC 29647
1-888-222-3525
www.parkseed.com

Pinetree Garden Seeds
Box 300
New Gloucester ME 04260
(207) 926-3400
www.superseeds.com

Seed Savers Exchange
3076 North Winn Road
Decorah IA 52101
seedsavers.org

Tomato Growers Supply Company
P. O. Box 2237
Ft. Meyers FL 33902
1-888-478-7333
www.tomatogrowers.com

Wayside Gardens
1 Garden Lane
Hodges SC 29695
1-800-845-1124
www.waysidegardens.com

Index

The New USDA Plant Hardiness Map

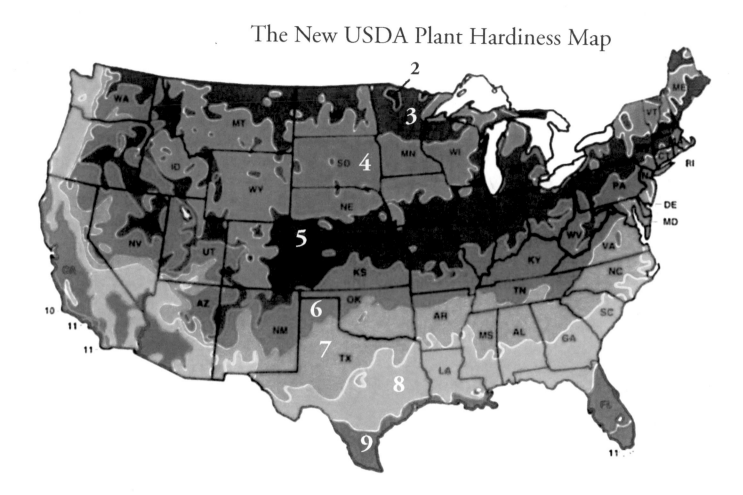

ZONE 1 Winter lows below -50°F. Sow seed in early spring when soil can be worked.

ZONE 2 Winter lows -50°F to -40°F. Sow seed in early spring when soil can be worked

ZONE 3 Winter lows -40°F to -30°F. Spring: April 15-June 15 — Fall: August 15-October 1

ZONE 4 Winter lows -30°F to -20°F. Spring: April 15-June 15 — Fall: September 1-October15

ZONE 5 Winter lows -20°F to -10°F. Spring: April 15-June 15 — Fall: September 1-October 15

ZONE 6 Winter lows -10°F to 0°F. Spring: March 15-May 15 — Fall: September 15-November 1

ZONE 7 Winter lows 0°F to 10°F. Spring: February 15-April115 — Fall: September 15-November 15

ZONE 8 Winter lows 10°F to 20°F. Spring: January 15-March 1 — Fall: October 1-December